D1709389

Walled Gardens

Walled Gardens

JULES HUDSON

National Trust

'Kings, Princes, and the wisest men of all ages, have some or other
of them, taken singular delight in this exercise of planting, setting,
sowing, and what else that is requisite in the well ordering of orchards
and gardens, and rejoiced to see the fruits of their labours.'

Leonard Meager, *The New Art of Gardening*, 1697

To the gardens and gardeners, past and present,
whose time and knowledge have been so freely given,
such that future generations might learn from their
labours and share in the endeavour of making the
best use of these enchanted spaces.

For Tania and Jack

CONTENTS

PAGES 2–3 The stunning borders in the kitchen garden at Felbrigg Hall in Norfolk reveal what enticing and productive places revived walled gardens can be. RIGHT The Italian garden enclosed by the once Lost Gardens of Heligan serves to introduce an element of exotic design in this now famously productive space.

INTRODUCTION

I saw my first walled kitchen garden nearly 30 years ago. It was small, ruinous and unkempt, and was attached to a small farmhouse in North Wales. As a young archaeology student I was part of a team surveying the wider prehistoric landscape nearby. For several weeks over a number of years in the early 1990s we camped within its crumbling walls as we went about our work.

Since that time I've developed a growing fascination for walled gardens, captivated by what I've long felt to be a curious contradiction. Walk into a vibrant and hard-working kitchen garden today and you'll be overwhelmed by the riot of colour and produce that stretches in every direction. Order and functionality underwrite this picture of beds and borders bursting with life – and yet, for all that sense of industry, they have always struck me as places that wrap you up in a comforting sense of calm. The door that separates the outside world from the one within is a complex, almost magical threshold. In crossing it you step into a space of enchantment, an escape from all that is burdensome in the world outside.

This is my own romantic view, of course. I'm sure that for many of the thousands of walled gardeners who worked their plots over the last 200 years or so, there were times when their gardens seemed anything but enchanted. Yet talk to the men and women who look after our revived walled kitchen gardens today and it is evident that, for all the hard graft their gardens require, none of them would trade where they work for anywhere else. There clearly is something special that life within such a surreal enclosure can conjure.

The walled kitchen garden of the past developed to such an extent that it did not only provide fruit, vegetables and flowers for a sophisticated country house, regardless of the season. Walled gardens also evolved into places of scientific endeavour, which through their development championed the invention of huge heated glasshouses and other innovative growing techniques. The crystal halls that

ABOVE LEFT The Dutch water gardens at Westbury Court in Gloucestershire are a rare example of a late seventeenth-century garden. Its walled gardens and canals were restored during the 1970s.

LEFT Glasshouses were a common feature of our greatest walled kitchen gardens, as here at Greenway in Devon, a house made famous as the home of Agatha Christie.

ABOVE The beautifully restored garden at Normanby Hall in Lincolnshire has been developed into a superb example of a Victorian kitchen garden bursting with life and colour.

allowed the production of rich and exotic fruits came to reflect the vast extent of Britain's empire, and the confidence that it inspired. For their owners and gardeners, such glasshouses were as much status symbols as vital food sources, and their design and construction mirrored the horticultural, social and architectural ambition of their creators.

I came to the task of writing a book on walled kitchen gardens not as a horticultural expert, but as an enthusiastic amateur and keen domestic gardener. Since my interest in walled gardens began three decades ago I have seen many more examples, often forlorn and forgotten – yet over the last 20 years a growing number have been resurrected and become productive once again. Of these, perhaps the once famously Lost Gardens of Heligan is the best-known example, in many ways blazing a trail of creative and commercial inspiration that others soon followed. Many walled gardens are in the care of the National Trust, such as Knightshayes Court, Attingham Park and the recently revived garden at Blickling Hall in Norfolk. To these can be added an increasing number of beautiful gardens in private or other hands, showing that today the fortunes of several of our greatest walled kitchen gardens are on the way back up – even as many still wait to be rescued.

Writing a book on the subject is not a new idea. My efforts follow in the footsteps of Susan Campbell, among others. Her tireless passion not only in highlighting the plight of so many forgotten gardens, but also in sharing her own hard-learnt understanding of how they worked, helped to inspire my own fascination with these spaces. For me, the role our nation's walled gardens played in furthering horticultural science, practice and architectural ambition puts them at the heart of gardening in Britain over the last 300 years.

Having enjoyed and absorbed the available sources, there came a point when I felt I knew enough to want to explore them for myself. So began a journey that would take me to many of our greatest kitchen

gardens. I was able to look at them afresh, learning from both the gardens and their gardeners, while sharing my own experience as a landscape and building historian. In travelling the country and immersing myself in the subject I have learnt a great deal. Like so many endeavours, however, the apparent completion of both book and journey serves only to remind me of how much more there is to discover.

There are, of course, thousands of walled kitchen gardens all over the country. Many are small and simple, little more than walled enclosures without the rich accessories of their more opulent cousins. My travels have focused on the biggest, for the principal reason that where these have been renovated they often preserve many of the most fascinating and diverse features to be found within a major walled garden. But I have also seen, and enjoyed, several more modest examples, and continue to do so as I explore the countryside during a busy filming year. Like so many secrets, once revealed and you know what to look for, walled gardens seem to crop up everywhere.

My physical journey through this fascinating subject reflects the voyage of discovery that this book seeks to convey. Starting out as an interested amateur, yet armed with the background of a former archaeologist, I soon realised that very little was known about the gardens themselves, often in contrast to the amount of information about the house and family they were built to support. As I started to visit yet more gardens, there appeared far more scope for a fresh appraisal of how many had evolved over the centuries.

LEFT Wonderfully productive espaliered fruit trees grow against the bricks of many walled gardens, such as this one at Gordon Castle in Moray.

RIGHT The entrance to the walled garden at Osterley Park in Middlesex. Behind the grand Robert Adam remodelling of the estate, its kitchen garden reveals a hint of earlier Tudor origins.

Where such studies had been made, as at Blickling and most recently at Berrington, they were of great value. Elsewhere I often found myself alongside the head gardener on an exhilarating hunt, exploring their gardens with a fresh eye, armed with whatever maps, plans and other sources came to hand. Having a professional background in historical research meant that on many occasions my guides and I were able to reinterpret the broad structural timeline of a garden by looking again at the history, brickwork and other archaeological clues, while drawing upon experience gained in the growing number of gardens I'd seen. Without doubt this book could not have been written without the very generous amounts of time, enthusiasm and good humour that my garden visits always enjoyed from the head gardeners, their colleagues and occasionally the owners who showed me around them. It was a great privilege to have had the opportunity to share their world on so many occasions, and to have always left feeling inspired.

As the research unfolded, it also became clear that many gardens shared features which, when taken together, described the anatomy of a walled kitchen garden. None had every possible feature available, but I feel all those chosen for inclusion here bring something unique and revealing to the overall story. I have therefore set out a broad guide of what to look for. I hope this will help anyone who shares my fascination for these beautiful places to develop their own understanding of them, just as I have done.

Like any book, *Walled Gardens* cannot hope to cover every aspect of what is, I have discovered, a huge and captivating subject – nor could I hope to visit every good example in the country. What to leave out can be a harder decision than what to put in. I have endeavoured to include what I believe to be some of the best representative examples, loosely organised chronologically. In understanding how the gardens were used, I learnt that much gardening practice is open to interpretation: what worked in one walled garden may not have been successful in another. However, it is their distinctive properties that make Britain's walled gardens such interesting places to explore. No two are ever the same; each has its own unique story and features. Yet together they record an exciting and revealing horticultural and social history that leads from the simple enclosures of the Middle Ages to the farthest corners of the British Empire. Across the centuries both gardeners and owners sought to create their own sense of Eden. In these enchanted worlds they could be surrounded by order, beauty and the finest fruits and vegetables from across the known world.

OPPOSITE William Fox Talbot, the pioneering Victorian photographer, would no doubt have taken inspiration from his kitchen garden at Lacock Abbey in Wiltshire.

BELOW At Gordon Castle in Moray, huge swathes of growing space are skilfully combined with contemporary design, including these striking crescent-shaped landforms.

PAGES 12–13 The unmistakable layout of the walled Flower Garden at Heligan looking north, with immaculate beds and borders now overlooked by the restored Paxton glasshouse (top left) and peach house on the right.

PART ONE

WALLED GARDENS IN
TIME AND SPACE

1 The walled garden through history

Walled kitchen gardens are a treat to explore, as here through the meandering herb garden at Acorn Bank in Cumbria. Although each example is unique, they all share common features that once recognised can help chart a garden's development, often in the absence of detailed records.

One of the frustrations in seeking to understand a specific garden's history is that it will usually have been far less well documented or recorded than that of the history of the house and family it once supported. Who were the walled kitchen gardeners of the past and why did they build what, in many cases, became such lavish enclosures?

These days we tend to celebrate the grandest examples, usually because they have been painstakingly reconstructed and contain the most interest. With immaculate beds and borders, and boasting a impressive range of glasshouses and other delights, the value of a rejuvenated kitchen garden is clear. Thousands of people now visit them every year and enjoy their produce in restaurants and cafés. It is from these thriving ranks that the gardens in this book are drawn. But in setting the privileged few in context, we need to consider the role of others, today silent and largely forgotten. The majority of Britain's walled kitchen gardens were modest affairs, probably less than 1 acre (0.4ha) in size and often adjacent to the house they supported – in stark contrast to the biggest, which were often relocated and enlarged as fashions and fortunes changed.

Drive through the countryside and you'll soon recognise plenty of these simple gardens alongside farmhouses, rectories and the elegant homes of minor aristocracy. Most that survive are now derelict, although others still soldier on as much cherished and productive private gardens. Yet barely a century ago these gardens would have numbered thousands. While most were little more than a large vegetable patch surrounded by a brick wall, with an occasional greenhouse leant up against it, collectively they played an invaluable role in feeding the nation and nurturing the development of horticultural skills.

From their inception walled gardens were a wholly practical addition, relied upon to produce enough fruit and vegetables to support large or small households throughout the year. They were, in effect, the private supermarkets of those who built and worked them: a vital food source expected to repay the investment required to build them. Over a period of 400 years the biggest and wealthiest estates took the simple concept of a walled kitchen garden and transformed it, both in size and capability. Among wealthy owners the ambition to out-produce their rivals established a horticultural arms race. This culminated in the great walled kitchen gardens of the late nineteenth and early twentieth centuries which championed the art, craft and science of gardening.

Perhaps one of the great fascinations with walled kitchen gardens is how their development came to reflect Britain's wider history, both at home and abroad. From the sixteenth century to the early twentieth, many of Britain's finest walled kitchen gardens were developed into centres of horticultural excellence, fuelled by their owners' ambitions and their gardeners' skills. Yet often so little is known about the detailed history of many individual gardens, they tempt the historical detective in us all to piece together their story.

As functional features which time and lack of resources eventually stripped of purpose, often little attention has been given to unravelling the pattern and pace of these gardens' evolution – yet such a timeline, once established, can reveal much about the changing fortunes of an estate. In many respects the walled kitchen garden, requiring as it did continual investment and development, became a significant reflection of its owner's financial success and horticultural ambition.

Kitchen gardens come in a range of shapes and sizes, often dictated by their position within the landscape. The uniquely terraced gardens at Slebech Park in Pembrokeshire afford a stunning view of the Daugleddau estuary.

ORIGINS OF THE WALLED GARDEN

For thousands of years gardeners have sought to protect their crops and hard work from the worst of the weather, pests and thieves. The idea of securing a plot of ground within some sort of enclosure is common around the world throughout human history. Be it a modest wattle fence, a hedge or a swaggering 12ft (3.7m) brick wall, the evolution of the walled garden has always been based on a sense of separation from the outside world.

In its most basic form, the kitchen garden is a simple square plot, divided by two crossing paths that dissect the space into quarters. These quarters may themselves have been divided further, but this simple arrangement allowed for the effective management of the garden from the outset, establishing what should be planted where and, importantly, when. Eventually the impact of walls, along with the garden's aspect and its capacity to marshal heat and light, transformed a simple enclosure into a scientific arena in which great horticultural advances could be made. Like most complex ideas, however, its origins were simple.

The ancestral line of the walled garden reaches back to the Romans. They enjoyed two types of garden, the enclosed garden found in cities and open, informal villa gardens. Examples of city gardens have been found in the ruins of Pompeii and Herculaneum, including covered colonnades around the garden resembling a cloister. This influence indeed extended on to Benedictine monasteries and their cloisters; the Abbey of Cassino, built in 1070, was described as a 'paradise in Roman fashion' and included patterned gardens for contemplation. Benedictine communities were very land-oriented, nurturing livestock and bees and growing vegetables and flowers. As the difference between horticulture and agriculture developed, gardens specifically designed for kitchen and medicinal use emerged.

ABOVE Taken from *The Gardener's Labyrinth*, published in 1571, this simple kitchen garden is surrounded by a wooden palisade, with an inner walk overlooking the central beds. A well to the left stands opposite an arbour.

RIGHT The beautifully ordered beds and glasshouses at Scotney Castle in Kent complement this fairy-tale estate, now centred around its much-embellished medieval tower. However, the 1 acre (0.4ha) walled gardens remain true to their origins.

EARLY WALLED GARDENS

The *hortus conclusus* or 'enclosed garden' of medieval Europe is a direct descendant from those of the abbeys; it was more typically enclosed by hedges or fencing. While not specifically a walled garden, the principle of offering protection from weather and straying animals had been established.

By the sixteenth century the landowning gentry and burgeoning middle class found themselves able to spend more of their resources on pleasure and comfort, rather than on self-defence and other essentials. Nevertheless, gardens of this period were almost always enclosed in some way, whether by walls, hedges, fences or moats. Walled gardens were meant to be seen and admired by those fortunate enough to be admitted; they were designed to be beautiful as well as productive. The 'cook's garden' could be hedged with hawthorn, and wattle hurdles or paled fencing were frequently used to create garden or land boundaries. Wealthier households used brick for walled 'pleasure grounds'.

Earlier Tudor gardens were in most cases relatively small in area. That at Blickling Hall, for example, began as no more than an acre (0.4ha), but as the fortunes of an estate and its owners fluctuated, so might the walled garden change and expand. The walls within early gardens were relatively unencumbered too, with the need to do little else but provide a secure boundary; as a result they were often lower than walls constructed in the eighteenth and nineteenth centuries. All in all, the walled garden of the late sixteenth or seventeenth century was a modest and simple element within an estate. It was very much a part of the domestic architectural format, together with the stables and other ancillary buildings.

Covering 3½ acres (1.4ha), the walled kitchen gardens at Felbrigg Hall in Norfolk are jewels in the National Trust's horticultural crown. Dominated by an iconic hexagonal dovecote, the gardens here are abundant, with an array of surviving glasshouses, fruit trees and root and salad crops, all retained within striking high walls.

As the Tudor and, later, Elizabethan manor house developed, the walled kitchen garden established itself as an essential component. Its main purpose was to provide a reliable source of fruit and vegetables for much of the year. More graceful architectural styles took the place of fortified castles, celebrating the idea of a garden as both a recreational space and a productive area. The emerging walled kitchen garden may have been a utilitarian arena, but this did not mean that it was regarded as something to hide. Gardens of the fifteenth and sixteenth centuries were usually attached to the main house in such a way that they helped to frame it – in effect extending the aspect of each elevation they bordered. They also afforded space to walk, reflect and enjoy the thriving garden.

In general, the Elizabethan walled kitchen garden combined great productivity with beauty and order. Such principles, once established, were to shape the development of the kitchen garden through time.

A glorious display of delphiniums within the walled garden at Felbrigg Hall, Norfolk.

THE GARDENER'S LABYRINTH AND OTHER SOURCES

In Britain, several published guides survive from the sixteenth and seventeenth centuries that set out the methods and practices required to build and run a walled kitchen garden effectively. One of the earliest was *The Gardener's Labyrinth*, written by Thomas Hill under the pseudonym 'Didymus Mountain' in 1577. Often drawn from much earlier classical sources, these early gardening guides offer a tantalising glimpse into the distant history of the walled garden and its origins overseas. The ancient texts upon which these works relied were preserved within monastic libraries, and would themselves have informed kitchen gardening techniques within abbeys and religious houses. From the pedigree of these sources we might reasonably infer that aspects of what we consider to be traditional 'British' walled kitchen gardening may well have been as popular with the Romans or those in medieval times as they were with Victorians.

This woodcut from the 1594 edition shows the planting of raised, possibly hot beds below, while at the top we see gardeners at work attending to trained fruit trees based upon a supporting framework, within a modest yet effective garden wall.

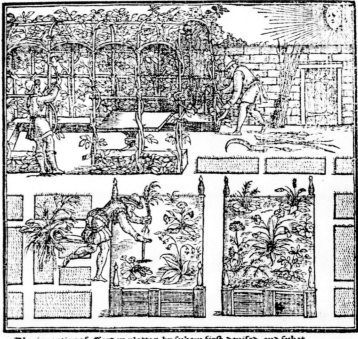

The Gardeners Labyrinth.

Contayning the manifolde trauayles, great cares, and diligence, to be yearly bestowed in euery earth, for the vse of a Garden: With the later inuentions, and rare secretes thereunto added (as the like) not heretofore publisthed.

The inuention of Garden plottes, by whom first deuised, and what commoditie founde by them, in time past.   Chap. 1.

He worthie Plinie (in his xix. booke) reporteth, that a Garden plotte in the Auncient time at Rome, was none other, than a small ½ simple inclosure of ground, whiche through the labour and diligence of the husbandmā, yeelded a commoditie and yearely reuenew vnto him . But after yeares (that man more estee=
A   med

It is precisely because the early garden was a catalyst for development that so few remain to be seen and understood. No matter how dressed and beautiful a kitchen garden may have been, it was ultimately a functional space. Since these early examples were first built, most have been either demolished or so redesigned that it is today virtually impossible to see an original example of an 'early English' walled garden.

Great social and horticultural change drove the development of the modest late medieval walled garden toward the classic walled kitchen garden we recognise today. During the seventeenth century, notwithstanding the effects of a decade of Civil War halfway through it, there emerged a growing squirearchy. Its interests at home and overseas would ignite a rapid expansion and investment in walled gardens, alongside the building of bigger and more impressive houses and estates. This new class of landed gentry, whose fortunes were often founded on widening global trade interests such as the growth of sugar plantations in the West Indies, brought wealth, investment and increasingly exotic horticultural tastes to Britain.

The house and lawned terrace at Acton Scott in Shropshire. There can be little doubt that when originally built this would have been a well-structured vegetable garden, located and designed to be enjoyed from the house.

FRUITS OF THEIR LABOURS

The first pineapple seen in England, brought from South America, is said to have been shown to Cromwell in 1657. Soon efforts were made to grow such highly prized fruits in England, or at the very least to sustain pre-potted examples shipped over from their equatorial countries of origin. Melons too became a popular staple, and walled gardeners were challenged to create artificial conditions of heat and light all year round. The new ways of responding to these challenges soon defined the successful walled garden as one that could remain consistently productive. On large estates a growing range of bespoke glasshouses were able to maintain native and exotic fruits to dress the finest dinner tables, even in the depths of winter.

During the sixteenth and seventeenth centuries the kitchen garden also produced a wide variety of plants for culinary, medicinal, cosmetic or veterinary use. Plants had been added over the centuries, firstly from Europe and the Mediterranean, then further afield from North Africa and Turkey and subsequently, via the Silk Road, from the Indian subcontinent and the borders of Asia. Later in the period, exploration of the New World instigated the arrival of a new influx of seeds and plants. The development of the enclosed garden with its warmer microclimate assisted the growing of these new vegetables, such as maize, potatoes, tomatoes and beans, although they were often used as ornamentals rather than crops.

GARDENS OF THE REVOLUTION

By the turn of the eighteenth century, the walled gardens that we see today were beginning to take shape alongside early Georgian, neoclassical country houses that were both graceful and sumptuous. Against this now familiar image of the country house estate, the fortunes of the walled garden accelerated. Early gardens were replaced or expanded to meet greater demands, making use of materials such as brick.

Despite its expense, brick soon became the material of choice for walls. These were now built higher and longer to better capture what heat the sun could provide, and to create a bigger growing area, particularly on the south-facing elevation. The natural heat retention properties of brick were recognised as its greatest virtue, leading to the development of the 'hot wall' around 1710. The use of heat, and later glass, to extend the growing year and mitigate the worst of the winter weather is a theme that pervades the development of the walled kitchen garden. In effect, walled gardeners of the past strove to bridge the gap in productivity that traditionally separated autumn and spring, seeking to prolong the growing season artificially.

It was during the second half of the eighteenth century that the walled garden underwent its most profound period of development. This was the period in which it was transformed from practical necessity to status symbol. There can be little doubt that the walled garden was always a source of pride among the larger and wealthier estates, their owners and gardeners. However, by the end of the eighteenth century the investment in the creation of walled gardens scaled new heights, with far-reaching consequences.

At the start of the century we might expect to find the walled garden close to, if not attached to, the house which it served. The subsequent revolution in landscape design, perhaps most famously associated with Lancelot 'Capability' Brown and Humphry Repton, set in motion a wholesale redesign of entire estates and their constituent parts. Older Elizabethan styles were replaced with an idealised vision of a classical landscape, of the sort that contemporary landscape painters were also trying to conjure. Out went the formal, geometric gardens that would once have surrounded a house over many acres. They were replaced with more informal, naturalistic planting schemes that sought to imitate a rural idyll, in which the landscape itself lapped at the doors and neoclassical porticos of the greatest country houses.

The basis for this radical change in trends was created in part by an explosion of interest in classical antiquity. The so-called 'Age of Enlightenment' of the late seventeenth and early eighteenth centuries witnessed rapid growth in the arts, sciences, literature and architectural modes of expression. The Grand Tour, the eighteenth-century equivalent of a gap year (it could last several), became a popular rite of passage for the (mainly) sons of the aristocracy, sent to gain a classical education among the ruins of Rome and the sophisticated hotspots of Paris, Florence and elsewhere. Inspired by the

The main
kitchen garden
at Calke Abbey
in Derbyshire is
now laid to lawn.
However, the
adjacent early
19th century
flower garden with
its semicircular
wall, flower house
and aviary, and
the neighbouring
physic garden
complete with
a stove house,
vinery and back
shed range are a
fine sight from the
air. It seems likely
this was once a
more lavish frame
yard, the whole
complex eventually
complemented
by the striking
orangery in the
centre.

architectural highlights of ancient Europe, they brought back many ideas and an even greater number of souvenirs, from paintings to sculptures and furnishings. Their appetite for all things classical also extended to more simple and timeless landscapes, tastes which a new and imaginative generation of British gardeners and designers were keen to accommodate.

This new genre of gardeners enjoyed great success and some, such as 'Capability' Brown, even obtained the patronage of the king and his court. For those in the market for a remodelled or 'improved' landscape about their estate, money seems rarely to have been an issue. As well as redesigning or even rebuilding a house, the plans put forward by these innovative landscapers required the removal or screening of anything that did not fit with their plan – and the walled garden was often top of the list.

Many walled gardens were thus demolished and relocated far from the house. This occurred both on aesthetic grounds, as the high walls would interfere with vistas, and for practical concerns: the comings and goings of a larger workforce meant that the scale and intensity of activity could be disruptive to the tranquil idyll of the new-look country house.

Relocation of walled gardens brought opportunities to create optimum growing conditions for fruit, vegetables and flowers. The lessons of the past were incorporated into the choice of new sites and materials used. Proximity to water and fertiliser (in the form of manure), shelter from the elements and fertility of the soil were fully exploited, resulting in an explosion of new structures and techniques. The gardens themselves were often screened by pleasure grounds of woodland planting; these led the visitor through the estate to a new, improved, walled kitchen garden, now a destination in its own right. The reinvented garden combined the industry of its workforce with the calm order and beauty of more honed design and management, even as its often greater size reflected the improved fortunes of family and estate.

Sweltering under the summer sunshine, the recently reconstructed kitchen gardens at Blickling Hall in Norfolk do great justice to the magnificent backdrop of the Jacobean house, once home to the young Anne Boleyn.

LEFT The pear alley seen from the central dipping pond at Beningbrough Hall, Yorkshire. Order and symmetry may have been kitchen garden essentials, but imagination was also a key ingredient, lending beauty to the garden's industry and purpose.

ABOVE The stable range at Osterley Park in south-west London was well sited next to the kitchen garden, ensuring a steady source of manure all year round.

The eighteenth century saw Britain's empire extended as far as India and witnessed an explosion in science and manufacturing that generated the Industrial Revolution. By the end of the century walled kitchen gardens had been relocated and re-equipped with heated walls, mushroom houses, bothies, root stores and cold frames, while the principles of earlier seventeenth-century orangeries were extended to encompass the design and production of glasshouses. The advent of the pinery and vinery, built specifically for the growing of pineapples and grapes, helped British gardens to catch up with established European growers, many of whom had already developed extensive glass structures in which to grow exotic fruits and native varieties through the winter. Most fine new gardens of the 1780s and '90s were now equipped with all these innovations. They successfully grew a huge array of vegetables and fruits, the most exotic of which reflected not just the extent of Britain's empire, but also the increasing appetite for horticultural science in the drawing rooms, libraries and nearby gardens of the landed classes.

The abundant walled garden at Beningbrough Hall, North Yorkshire.

GARDENS IN THE AGE OF EMPIRE

The accession of Queen Victoria to the throne in 1837 began a period in history that has since defined the nineteenth century. By the time she was crowned the threat posed by France, not just to Britain, but to all of Europe, had ended, defeated at the battle of Waterloo in 1815. Social reform was making gradual progress and the Industrial Revolution continued to transform Britain's landscape, as first canals and then railways began to connect new towns and cities from the clay and coalfields of Wales and the Midlands to London and the major ports.

This explosion of manufacturing created a new and wealthy class of trader, many of whom sought to build their own family seats and estates complete with all the trappings, including walled kitchen gardens. The framework of walled gardens had been established at the end of the previous century, but it was Victorian ingenuity and continued investment from both new and old money that led to their heyday. Improvements in steam technology, boilers and the introduction of hot water heating systems to glasshouses all helped those who could afford it to indulge their passion for plants and horticulture.

In 1845 the glass tax was abolished. Since its introduction in 1745, this punitive tax had sought to exploit the wealthy by making glass a taxable luxury, along with a window tax (1696–1851). Because glass was charged for by weight, the effect in terms of glazing was to make it thinner and more brittle, which had a direct impact on the design and cost of glasshouses. Both the glass tax and the longer-running window tax greatly hampered glass development and production until both had been successfully repealed.

Three years after the abolition of the glass tax, plate glass was invented, and not long after that the window tax was abolished. As a result the cost of glass plummeted. The costs of glasshouses fell further during the second half of the century, as increasing numbers of bespoke manufacturers honed mass production techniques. The future of the walled garden as a status symbol, and the principal food source for the estate, was assured.

DECLINE AND FALL

By the start of the twentieth century the prospects for Britain, her empire, the ruling classes, their estates and walled gardens seemed secure. Britannia ruled the waves and British manufacturing had an imperial marketplace in which to prosper. But the First World War, which began in the late summer of 1914 and ground on for over four years, transformed the nature of British society and the aspirations of those who had sustained it. The enormous workforce required by the country's biggest estates had, by the early 1920s, been increasingly liberated from a lifetime of service. Many skilled gardeners had been lost during the war, and many who returned sought more lucrative employment.

The First World War was the first really industrialised war, and it relied on huge quantities of imports from abroad. The Merchant Navy developed the means to transport food from all over the world. Imported goods were increasingly available to all, and the niche provision of produce by Britain's

walled gardens began to falter. As estates began to feel a squeeze on staffing from both lower incomes and higher wages, the ability of many to justify such expense began to wane. Heligan in Cornwall, abandoned soon after the First World War, is a good example of the trend. Others continued, some, such as Attingham Park, even enjoying further investment, but the eventual decline of the walled kitchen garden was inevitable. Despite a brief resurgence during the Second World War, when glasshouses were used to produce food for the home front, by the 1960s many had fallen into disuse, their once immaculate and ordered beds and borders now overgrown or grassed over. Prized glasshouses lay empty and at the mercy of the elements, while in the face of crippling post-war death duties many of the houses they once served were demolished, sold or entrusted to charitable care.

There were virtually no major walled gardens in operation anywhere in Britain by the late 1980s, highlighting how quickly these once immaculate spaces could disappear if left untended. Yet just a few years later, in the early 1990s, simultaneous projects got underway within the National Trust and elsewhere, notably around the now famous Lost Gardens of Heligan. Such ambitious reconstruction projects set in train a steady revival of Britain's walled kitchen gardens. The schemes not only rediscovered the knowledge and means of saving them, but also crucially established the public appetite to do so. Today many walled gardens are again flourishing, demonstrating what productive places they can be.

OPPOSITE The dilapidated glasshouses now virtually lost within the walled gardens at Plas Newydd, Anglesey represent the fate of most kitchen gardens by the end of the twentieth century. Yet with care and investment, they could once again be returned to use.

LEFT Gardens are nothing without their gardeners. Old tools, last put down decades ago, can offer a tantalizing sense of days gone by, as here among the abandoned gardens at Plas Newydd in Anglesey.

2 The anatomy of the walled kitchen garden

The imposing and elegant gateway to the walled garden at Hinton Ampner, Hampshire. Not all walled gardens had such grand thresholds, but they all mark the boundary between the world outside and the productive and enchanting realm within.

READING A WALLED GARDEN

To understand the development and history of a walled kitchen garden, we need to recognise its key features and date them with some degree of certainty. We also need to spot and decipher any distinct phases of construction hidden within its plan or fabric, drawing these threads together to chart its development. Throughout the life of a garden many elements once vital to its success as the productive hub of an estate or farm will have been added or removed, embellished or discarded. These architectural and horticultural features can help us interpret the historic timeline of a garden, particularly for those dating from the eighteenth century or before. Piecing together even the most basic sequence of building can transform our vision of how a garden was planned, used, developed and regarded over its lifetime.

Walled gardens across Britain share many features that tell their stories over the centuries, but it is rare that one example has them all. Yet in being able to distinguish a mushroom house from a fruit store, or an expensive brick wall from an earlier stone one, or to appreciate that the peach house or vinery was a later addition, we can begin to chart the pattern of investment in a garden. In so doing we gain insight into how the garden was valued by those who owned, built and subsequently maintained it.

Understanding these features and making sense of how they were employed can help us to *read* a garden more effectively. For me, it is the process of connecting the often scant documentary history with the surviving built archaeology and then interpreting it that makes the exploration of walled kitchen gardens so fascinating. But where is best to start?

The walled garden at Attingham Park in Shropshire is one of the most complete and compelling examples in the country, possessing many of the major features seen in other well-developed kitchen gardens.

THE FANTASY WALLED GARDEN

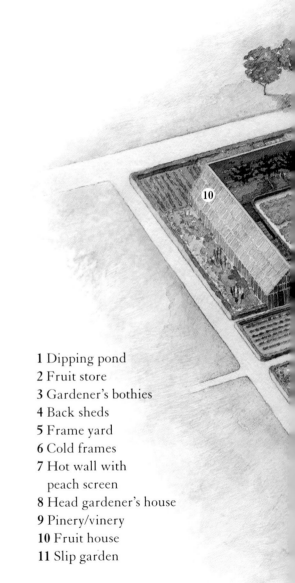

The easiest way to begin to understand how any walled garden may have developed is to establish a basic plan of what the perfect and most complete walled garden *might* have looked like. In bringing the key features together, it is possible to create a *fantasy* walled kitchen garden that, had it ever existed, would have showcased the finest attributes any could have wished for.

Our fantasy garden was built during the heyday of the walled kitchen garden at the turn of the twentieth century. It represents a plan designed with the benefit of at least 150 years of hindsight. This garden did not simply evolve, unlike so many from the eighteenth century and before. Instead, as with other late nineteenth-century examples, its position and layout were crafted on the drawing boards of experienced designers. They sought to combine many past lessons, ironing out the inefficiency of continued development and construction. New plans worked inwards, starting with the walled garden's position within the wider park and moving on to the location of the frame yards, an important industrial area given over to the day-to-day running of the garden, along with boiler houses and details of the smallest beds and borders. This template aims to provide an essential guide to make sense of any walled kitchen garden in the country.

No single walled kitchen garden survives that has all the features that might have been found in the perfect example. This fantasy garden has therefore been designed to demonstrate how most key elements might have been arranged if such a garden had existed, towards the end of the nineteenth century.

1 Dipping pond
2 Fruit store
3 Gardener's bothies
4 Back sheds
5 Frame yard
6 Cold frames
7 Hot wall with
   peach screen
8 Head gardener's house
9 Pinery/vinery
10 Fruit house
11 Slip garden

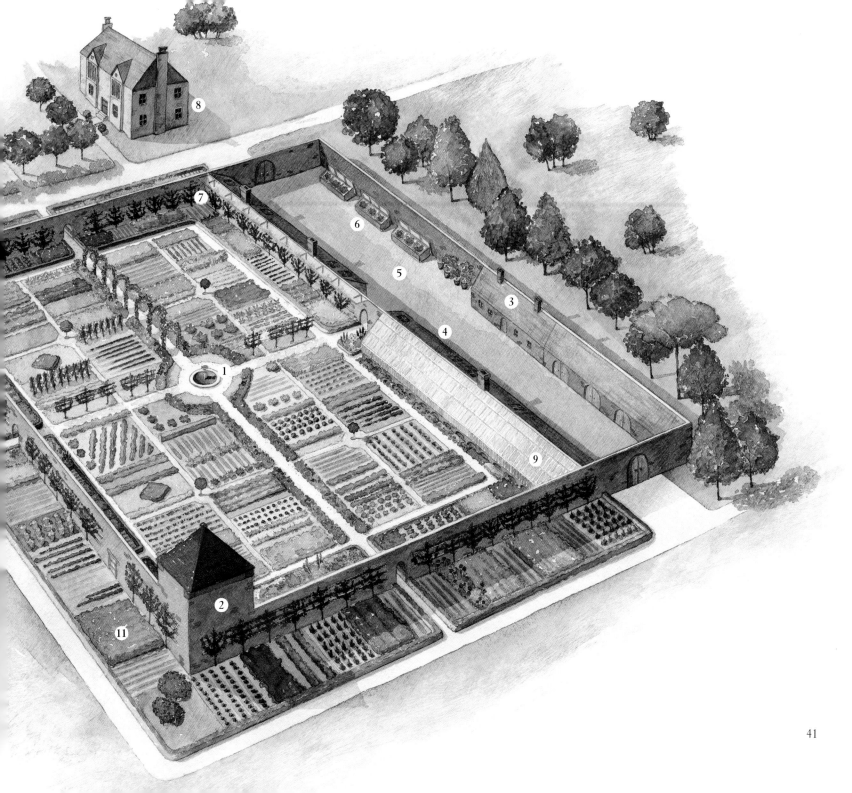

LOCATION

The first thing to consider with any walled kitchen garden is its location within the landscape that surrounds it, and its proximity to the house that it served. Walled gardens were among the most expensive components of an estate, and where early examples survive they tend to remain close to or adjacent to the main house.

Many of our greatest kitchen gardens were created during the eighteenth-century infatuation with 'improved' landscapes, a movement that continued to influence later Victorian practices. These gardens were now sited away from the house, hidden from view and screened by belts of trees and pleasure grounds. When looking at larger estates, the relationship between house and garden is therefore often the first clue in determining a garden's age, along with the history of the house and its owners. Smaller sites, such as farmhouses, larger Victorian rectories or the homes of the squirearchy often retained their kitchen garden nearby, as there was neither the need nor the financial capacity to landscape their surroundings in the same way. In these instances the garden remains as a functional and practical addition, echoing the earlier origins of the kitchen garden in the fifteenth and sixteenth centuries.

Gravetye Manor, Kent. The Elizabethan house retained an original walled garden adjacent to it until the late nineteenth century, when William Robinson replaced it with a flower garden, building a new, uniquely elliptical kitchen garden further away. Nonetheless, Robinson was following a convention established in the eighteenth century, when many walled gardens were relocated away from the house they served.

43

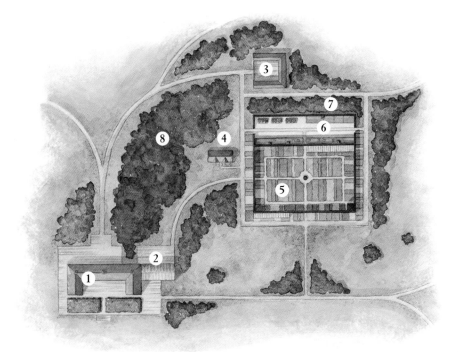

This illustration sets out in broad terms the position of the garden in relation to the main house, stable yard and wider park in our fantasy walled garden.

1 House
2 Orangery
3 Stable yard
4 Head gardener's house
5 Walled kitchen garden
6 Frame yard
7 Shelter belts
8 Pleasure grounds

'IMPROVED' LANDSCAPES

The desire to create the 'perfect' landscape during the eighteenth century under the auspices first of William Kent, then Lancelot 'Capability' Brown and later Humphry Repton, among others, had a profound and positive effect on the walled garden. Many earlier houses and their gardens were either demolished and re-sited. Others were so dramatically remodelled that trying to trace the location of the original garden in what may be an 'improved' eighteenth-century landscape can prove difficult, if not impossible. Only archival estate plans, maps and, where they exist, the detailed notes of their designers, such as those recorded in Repton's 'Red Books', may give some clue as to where an earlier kitchen garden on an estate might have been, if one existed at all. Gardens were not the only disposable item on the landscapers' list; villages and even churches could be moved if the ultimate view demanded it.

The wholesale relocation of kitchen gardens at this time is significant not simply as a gauge of changing trends. It usually resulted in a better position and an increase in size for walled gardens, reflecting not just the family's improving fortunes, but also a greater understanding of horticultural demands. A successful garden was increasingly expected to provide both traditional staples and a growing range of imported exotics throughout the year.

SHELTER BELTS

In the 1925 edition of the *Gardener's Assistant*, that weighty work which has been both friend and guide to gardeners since 1859, it is noted that:

Walls afford good shelter when there is little wind, and that steady; but when there is much it eddies around the inside of the walls, and produces far more injurious effects on the vegetation it meets on its course than it does on that not subjected to intermittent excitement.

The 'excitement' referred to was further compounded by prevailing cold winds – the reason why many walled gardens were complemented by higher shelter belts of trees, usually planted to the north and east. These woodland areas helped to mitigate the effects of strong and cold winds on the garden, in the same way that a breakwater disrupts the flow of a stormy sea. From the mid-eighteenth century onwards thick belts of trees, consisting of fast-growing evergreens or slower-growing native deciduous species such as spruce, larch, sycamore and beech, sought to protect the walled garden further. Where possible, the siting of the garden may have taken advantage of an existing copse or woodland, while others may have formed part of an overall planting plan for the wider landscaped park. Today these features are often obvious as they tower over the surrounding parkland, for example at Knightshayes in Devon or Clumber Park in Nottinghamshire. However, they would have required some vision and patience to appreciate when first planted, given how long the trees would take to mature and become effective.

This dramatic image of a rainbow piercing the eastern shelter belt behind the enormous gardens at Gordon Castle in Moray highlights just how much protection a well-sited patch of woodland can give.

SLIP GARDENS

From the mid-eighteenth century the land around major walled gardens was also prized as a profitable area for growing, as the beneficial effect of the walls extended to the outside beds. Offering varying degrees of shelter, these areas were known as slip gardens or 'slips'. They were well-suited to the growing of hardy root vegetables and fruit that did not require the all-round protection found within the garden. Slips tended to occupy the south, west and eastern fringes of a kitchen garden; corresponding walls were also covered in fruit trees or, occasionally, more glasshouses on the south-facing outer wall. The cooler northern slip was usually reserved for the business end of the garden, where compost, fuel, back sheds, bothies and, later, boiler rooms were located.

The eastern slip garden at Tyntesfield near Bristol is once again productive, with young fruit cordons adorning the walls, which date to the late eighteenth century.

SIZE

Of the many thousands of walled kitchen gardens that once existed, these days we tend to focus on the biggest and most important. The simple reason is that they are often associated with homes or organisations which, through commercial or charitable means, have had the opportunity to renovate them. Yet most were far more modest, perhaps covering no more than a quarter or half an acre (0.1–0.2 ha), attached to a farm or mid-sized country house. Mainly consisting of simple walled enclosures, such gardens may have had acquired a glasshouse in the late nineteenth or early twentieth century. Yet although never destined to be equipped with the array of features seen in the largest, these smaller gardens were informed by the horticultural advances made in more elaborate ones. They may not have been developed to the same scale, but are nevertheless invaluable elements in the broader story of the walled garden. The variety of size reminds us just how important was the walled garden's role in supporting rural families from the bottom of society to the top.

In considering the largest walled gardens, in 1859 the *Gardener's Assistant* suggested that 4 acres (1.6ha) was the optimum size for a kitchen garden supporting a reasonable estate. Comparable examples might include those at Weston Park in Shropshire or Tatton Park in Cheshire, although smaller gardens of around 2 acres (0.8ha) were usually sufficient, as at Attingham Park in Shropshire. At the other end of the scale the walled gardens at Welbeck Abbey, Nottinghamshire, built for the Duke of Portland, covered 20 acres (8ha), while the Royal Gardens at Windsor eventually spread to a staggering 30 acres (12ha).

However, size is only one indicator of a garden's value, and of the wealth of those who built it. Irrespective of how many acres it covered, the principle of growing produce all year round within the unique environment created by the garden's walls was common to all.

When seen from above, most working kitchen gardens appear enormous, as at Scotney Castle in Kent. Covering just a single acre (0.4ha), this example is relatively modest; most were double the size, while some, such as the one at Windsor Castle, eventually extended to 30 acres (12ha).

SHAPE

Most walled kitchen gardens were either roughly square or rectangular. The latter shape was favoured because it created a longer south-facing wall upon which to harvest the best of the sunshine. The relatively square corners also meant that the beds and borders could be arranged with some accuracy and symmetry.

However, as with most conventions, there were exceptions to the rule. At Attingham Park in Shropshire, a garden previously thought of as rectangular has now been recognised as being trapezoidal. Its south-facing wall is the longer side, making best use of its aspect, and the western wall comes a close second, designed to capture the last rays of the setting sun. The north-facing southern boundary is shorter still, while the eastern wall is the shortest of all. These details only came to light when restoration of the gardens required its gardeners to lay out the quarters once again – only to find that it was impossible to achieve an orderly right angle in relation to its towering walls.

There are good examples where garden designers seemed to go out of their way to challenge the accepted wisdom of the day. At Berrington Hall in Herefordshire, 'Capability' Brown created a spectacular curved south-facing wall, thus providing more wall space within the same width of garden. At Luton Hoo, Brown built a striking octagonal version, while his successor, Humphry Repton, also experimented with six- or seven-sided gardens, for example at Herriard in Hampshire. As late as 1901 William Robinson, the great Victorian garden writer and celebrated maverick, typically bucked conventional trends with his elliptical kitchen garden at Gravetye Manor in Kent.

Seen from above, the trapezoidal shape of the walled garden at Mottisfont in Hampshire is easily discernable.

ORIENTATION AND LAYOUT

It might be expected that the optimum orientation of a classic walled garden would be exactly north to south. Yet for many gardens, south-south-east facing, and located on a slight slope, gave the best results as it captured the full sun before midday. There are, of course, many other variations to be found around the country.

The first thing that strikes anyone entering a restored and productive kitchen garden is the vivid horizon of life and colour. Leading pathways beckon you on between regiments of canes and beans toward neat cages wrapped in netting. Tidy rows of salad crops and brassicas are framed by the backdrop of walls, covered in espaliered fruit trees. Below, swathes of herbs and other essential pollinators add colour and order, stretching out in every direction. From ground level, when a garden is in the full flush of early summer, it can be hard to recognise that underlying this rich harvest is

a clearly defined plan at the heart of the garden's success.

The traditional design of a walled kitchen garden – split into four quarters separated by paths, with a well-head or pool at the centre – dates back to the very earliest gardens of Persia (present-day Iran). The garden's quadrants, broadly reflecting the cardinal points of the compass, were formed with pathways running west to east and north to south, and often led to corresponding doorways within the walls. The quadrants could be further subdivided, but this basic structure allowed the walled gardener to manage a carefully planned rotation of crops throughout the beds year after year, resting a quadrant or sub-quadrant when required. Using this simple pattern, order and routine was established across what could have easily become a planting free-for-all.

Neat rows of vegetables at Attingham Park, Shropshire.

WALLS

Protecting produce from pests and the elements was the *raison d'être* of the walled garden, the majority of which had relatively modest walls of 8–10ft (2.4–3m) in height. Admittedly the walls of a large eighteenth- or nineteenth-century garden could reach up to 18ft (5.5m), but earlier examples were almost certainly smaller, as those at Easton Walled Gardens in Lincolnshire demonstrate.

The walls of the kitchen garden provide its character. In many cases they also offer a rich, if sometimes perplexing, series of clues to how a garden has been developed over time. Their size, and the area they encompass, along with the materials from which they are made, help to decipher the sequence of events that created a garden, even when a written history may be absent. Understanding how they were built and how, and why, they have been altered is an important aspect of a garden's story.

ABOVE LEFT The relatively modest height of the walls at Easton Walled Gardens in Lincolnshire were probably typical of many early kitchen gardens prior to the eighteenth century.

LEFT The south-facing wall at Llanerchaeron has been increasingly scarred over two centuries as successive glasshouses have been added and then replaced.

OPPOSITE Wisteria cascading over the garden wall at Barrington Court, Somerset. Below the wall is the canalised moat of the house.

MATERIALS

The materials used in the creation of the walls can vary across both time and place. It will come as no surprise to learn that, with the exception of later glasshouses, the walls of a kitchen garden were its most costly feature, regardless of size. The ambition of the walled gardener was to build both efficiently and effectively, but rarely, it appears, cheaply. The heat-absorbing properties of various materials, from stone to brick to cob (a mix of clay, dung and straw), were long recognised by gardeners as essential to the success of the walled garden. Of all materials available to the walled gardeners of the past, one was prized above all: the humble brick.

Most large kitchen gardens we see today were built from the eighteenth century onwards, and the best made good and extensive use of brick. It was not only easy to build with, but also retained heat exceptionally well, while the lime mortar that kept the walls stable was useful in accepting the nails needed to tie up and train espaliered fruit trees. The use of the walls to train fruit trees meant that supporting piers were mostly built to protrude on the outside, leaving the inner face free of obstruction, although in many examples this was not the case. However, where a garden has been extended over time, the presence of pillars on what appears to be the inside of walls may indicate that this was once an external face, subsequently incorporated into a bigger enclosure. It's also worth remembering that, prior to the mid-nineteenth

OPPOSITE
Perhaps one of
the most evocative
features to be
found in many
abandoned walled
gardens are the
rusty nails that
once supported
fruit trees, driven
into the mortar by
past generations of
gardeners.

century, brick was an expensive material that was also taxed; by the turn of the eighteenth century it had become a symbol of wealth for those who could afford to use it.

However, brick walls were not new to the eighteenth century. Brickmaking in Britain dates back to the Roman period, and enjoyed a revival in late medieval times. Differing patterns and sizes help to determine the age of the walls. 'English bond' is a course of stretchers (lengthways) bricks, with the next laid as headers (widthways); 'Flemish bond' from 1623 alternates headers and stretchers in the same course. Many other styles developed over the seventeenth century, including 'Sussex bond' (three stretchers between single headers per course) and 'rat trap' or 'Chinese bond' (bricks set on their edge, leaving a cavity in between). During the eighteenth century bricks were expensive, certainly in comparison with more readily available materials such as local stone, in places where this

RIGHT
Understanding
the range of brick
bonds used can
determine phases
of construction in
a garden, even if
the precise date
remains uncertain.
This is Flemish
bond, a simple
arrangement of
alternate headers
and stretchers.

53

existed naturally. Before mass brick production developed in the nineteenth century, along with the infrastructure of canals and, later, railways to transport it, the brick was extremely labour-intensive to make. The clay had to be sourced, then pressed into timber moulds by hand before being baked in quantity within large, purpose-built kilns. Estates often scoured their own land for deposits of clay, as at Llanerchaeron in west Wales. Here clay pits were mined and the bricks made on site by itinerant brick makers, who made a living travelling from job to job.

At Llanerchaeron, the wall is comprised of a mixture of stone for the outer, less visible and least productive northern face, and brick for the inside. This became a common and practical compromise, repeated in gardens across the country; Gordon Castle in Moray and Plas Newydd in Anglesey offer further examples. If money were no object, however, then bricks might be used throughout – an impressive demonstration of wealth that underlined the walled garden's new role as a status symbol.

BRICK TAX AND SERPENTINE WALLS

In 1784 the government of George III, having just been embroiled in a costly War of Independence in the American Colonies, introduced a tax on bricks. The tax was aimed at making good some of the losses from the war, but it had a profound effect upon Britain's building industry before repeal in 1850. By the time it was introduced bricks had long been favoured for the growing number of walled kitchen gardens being built. Under the new levy they were taxed at 4 shillings per thousand, leading brickmakers to increase the size of their bricks as a way of mitigating the tax. For the larger estates, more able to absorb the increased costs, the deliberate use of bricks became a symbol of prosperity and social status.

One subtle and economical way of using bricks was in the design of serpentine or crinkle-crankle walls. Their distinctive wavy lines meant they were inherently more stable, rarely requiring the addition of pillars because they were essentially self-supporting. As a result these walls could be made thinner, sometimes just one brick thick, and with around one-third less materials. Walls shaped in this way also had the advantage of more surface area within a set distance, very useful when training fruit trees up them. Although the use of serpentine walls dates back to the seventeenth century, it is thought that the large number found in East Anglia, for example at Melford Hall in Suffolk, may have been due to Flemish influence, following a large influx of Flemish settlers during the sixteenth century. Elsewhere in England, the walled kitchen garden at Deans Court in Dorset provides a fine example of a serpentine enclosure.

When the tax was finally lifted, brick manufacturing had become far more mechanised. An explosion in the use of bricks throughout the second half of the nineteenth century has since come to define Victorian architecture.

The unmistakable profile of a serpentine or crinkle-crankle wall. This superb example is from the kitchen garden at Deans Court in Dorset.

HOT WALLS

As the building of more elaborate and ostentatious walled gardens accelerated during the eighteenth century, so did the development and use of the 'hot wall'. The gardens at Croome Court in Worcestershire and Belvoir Castle in Nottinghamshire both claim to have the first examples, possibly as early as 1710, but whatever the truth of it they were certainly not the last.

The principle was simple; the wall was constructed with a long, horizontal, 'S'-shaped flue, spanning 10 or 20 feet (3–6m), hidden in its centre. At the bottom was a fire pit and at the top a chimney. When a fire was lit at the base, the warm air would heat the wall from within, enabling the brick to conduct the warmth through to the face of the wall. Trained along the wall were espaliered fruit trees, such as peaches, pears and nectarines. Heating the wall in this way, often with an array of flues, could help tender shoots survive early and late frosts. In my view the hot wall is one of the features that helped establish the walled kitchen garden as a hotbed of horticultural innovation.

Hot walls were occasionally retro-fitted, as at Packwood House, Warwickshire. Tucked away next to a corner tower, possibly a store, is a later fire pit under the arch. Note the lack of brick bonding between the earlier wall and the newer structure.

PLANTING SCHEMES AND PLANTS

The gardens of today that are once again productive are rarely able to copy any historic planting scheme. Limited records, allied to the need to grow crops relevant to their current objectives and staffing capacity, mean that the modern garden will never be able to recreate the look of its past exactly – nor, arguably, should it. Walled gardens remain as expensive to run as they always were, and generally no longer have the imperative for year-round production to justify large numbers of gardeners. Their role must adapt to the conditions under which they have been renovated.

As any gardener will tell you, gardens change with those who garden them, year after year, century after century. Successive generations of walled gardeners working right across the country were no exception. When seen overall, the story of the walled kitchen garden in Britain is one of change and development, making the task of selecting and recreating specific historic eras almost impossible – especially when an established garden may have evolved over 200 years. Nonetheless, all walled gardeners had to contend with, and take advantage of, several common features. These allowed them to make the best of what was always a unique and prized asset, within which they sought to exercise the best horticultural skill, judgement and innovation.

These conventions, when set out in plan, offer a helpful guide to understanding how many walled kitchen gardens might have been used. I have taken a simple rectangular garden as an example.

ABOVE These borders at Beningbrough Hall in North Yorkshire are a striking interpretation of what might have been planted in the past.

RIGHT A classic planting plan from *The Gardener's Assistant* (1925).

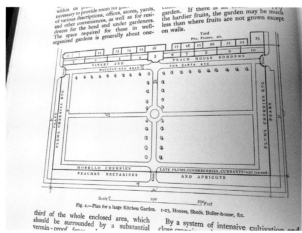

Within our fantasy walled garden, almost every type of fruit and vegetable was produced, along with numerous flowers and herbs. However, the areas of the garden in which key varieties of fruit and vegetables were planted are based upon a series of conventions that were common to many walled gardens across the country (see also pages 40–41).

1 Peaches, apricots, nectarines, figs
2 Early plums, apples, sweet cherries, figs
3 Pears
4 Hardy herbaceous and flowers
5 Fruit house
6 Morello cherries, late pears, gooseberries
7 Canes and beans
8 Espaliered fruit trees
9 Late plums, currants
10 Flower border
11 Pinery/vinery
12 Pears
13 Plums, early pears, greengages, cherries, apricots

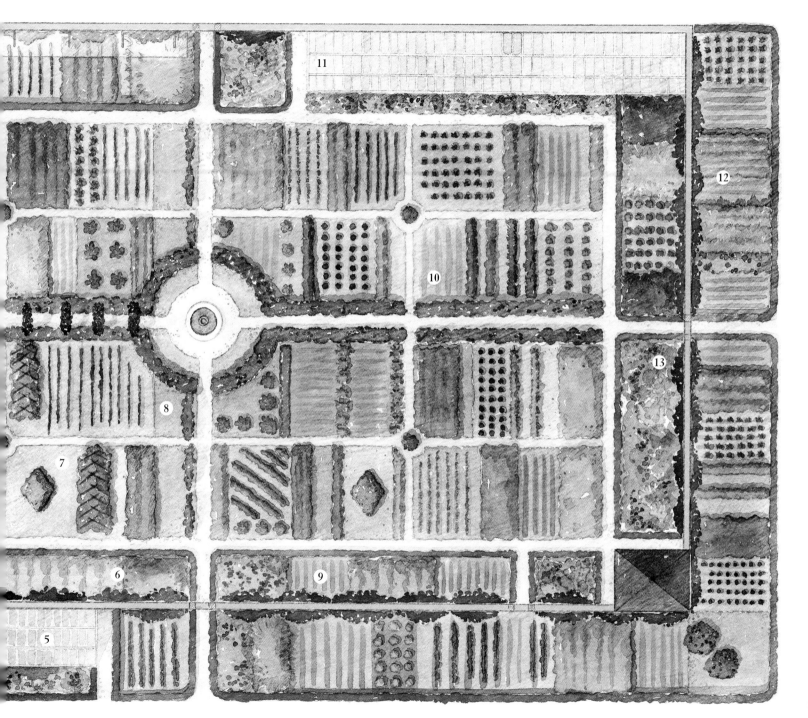

FRUIT WALLS

The increase in the size of kitchen gardens not only affected the area they occupied. The height of their surrounding walls also increased, driven not only by the emerging need to support lean-to glasshouses, but also to harness the value of growing fruit up walls. This technique enabled produce to absorb the heat of the sun by itself, to great effect.

The south-facing wall was, of course, the most prized and in many respects the most productive aspect. In later gardens this wall was almost always largely covered with glasshouses, or occasionally have been heated with internal flues as a 'hot wall'. Yet earlier or more modest gardens may have simply relied upon the natural passage of the sun. In its basic form, the south-facing wall was the perfect spot for peaches, nectarines, apricots and figs.

Moving clockwise, the internal face of the eastern wall was favoured for plums, early pears, greengages, cherries and apricots, which could bask in the warmth of the setting summer sun.

The inner, north-facing wall offered apparently uninviting temperatures at the bottom of the garden. It was also put to good use, however, being well suited to growing Morello cherries, late plums, gooseberries, currants, late pears and mulberries.

Finally, the western wall, with its easterly internal aspect, was often adorned with sweet cherries, figs, early plums and certain varieties of apple.

This arrangement is, of course, simply a guide, and different gardens across the country will have had their own variations. However, this layout forms the recognised basis for most walled kitchen garden renovations in recent years.

When trained through wire, iron or timber supports, espaliered fruit trees also provide great dividers within larger kitchen gardens, as here at Clumber Park, Nottinghamshire.

PEACH SCREENS

Frost was a recognised problem that could affect fruit trees, even those trained and pinned to the warmer, south-facing walls. With this in mind a simple design was eventually developed. A narrow canopy was mounted on iron brackets, which ran along the top or middle portion of the wall. This canopy, made from wooden planks or, latterly, glass panes, was only 18in (46cm) or so wide, yet the shelter it provided was sufficient to interrupt the fall of frost. As time went on the practice of hanging matting, tightly woven nets or, in some cases, elaborate glass panes – effectively creating a temporary greenhouse during the colder snaps – became common. Today many surviving walls still display remnant brackets as testament to their widespread use.

LEFT AND ABOVE This wall at Berrington Hall in Herefordshire still has its original cast-iron peach screen brackets. These inspired the creation of some stunning copies, which now line the walls of the much rebuilt kitchen garden at Newport House, also in Herefordshire.

ESPALIERED FRUIT TREES

The practice of pruning trees to grow them up walls or frames produced numerous styles of 'espaliered' tree. Taken from the Italian '*spalliera*', meaning 'something to rest the shoulder against', the term initially referred to the support or frame upon which the plant relied. Later it described the practice itself, then gave way in turn to other terms for particular styles; 'cordons', 'fans' and 'candelabra' are three of the more popular variations. Not only do the geometric patterns add texture to the wall; such hard and controlled pruning also creates an accessible plant that fruits evenly and efficiently. An alternative is the aptly named 'step-over' tree, pruned to provide a low barrier and create a border around a bed. Espaliered fruit trees remain a versatile and popular way of defining areas within a kitchen garden while also being productive in a minimal amount of valuable growing space.

TOP These candelabra examples at Tyntesfield in Somerset demonstrate how much interest, form and colour fruit trees can provide, in addition to their annual crop.

ABOVE These cordons at Tyntesfield give an idea of what the rest of its restored walls will look like when fully planted.

WHICH PLANTS?

Fashions in plants, as in everything else, come and go. The range of available seeds and varieties grew decade by decade, from artichoke gardens in the seventeenth century to the craze for pineapples in the eighteenth. By 1750, in addition to the usual vegetable crops and New World additions such as squashes and potatoes, the country gentleman could purchase kohlrabi, cardoons, sorrel, asparagus and multiple types of melon. The range was becoming extremely broad. Lettuces alone, for instance, could provide Rose, Red, Curl'd, Arabian, Versailles, Aleppo, Cos, Silesia or Black Spanish. By 1800 even local nurseries would stock up to 35 varieties of eating apples, 38 types of pear, 41 types of peaches, 13 grape varieties and seven types of fig to satisfy the gentry's passion for fruit. Varieties were developed with exotic names, such as Pear 'Joséphine de Malines' from 1830 and Plum 'Coe's Golden Drop' from 1790.

ABOVE A melon growing in the glasshouse at Clumber Park, Nottinghamshire.

RIGHT Competition is a great driver, and the need to prove horticultural excellence gave rise to many local, regional and national events. Willy Robertson, the former head gardener of Gordon Castle, Moray, enjoyed decades of success.

Crop rotation patterns were diligently followed, as they had been for centuries, in order to avoid a build-up of pests and diseases and depletion of the soil. The classic four-way rotation consisted of legumes followed by alliums, then roots and tubers followed by brassicas. By the late nineteenth century, identifying the seasons in which crops became mature had become an art form. The breeding of new hybrid varieties, clever cultivation techniques and skilful storage had extended the season, and the practice of simultaneous cropping had become standard. This was an extremely efficient method of cultivation in which crops with similar or symbiotic needs were grown together. Endives, for example, were planted on the banks produced by celery trenching; strawberry runners might be interplanted with onions in July before growing into the space when the onions were cleared for cropping the following year. Vegetables were specifically bred to crop at staggered times or for long periods. The head gardener would also ensure that by careful planning and planting specific varieties into cooler or warmer areas of the garden he could accelerate or slow down cropping on demand. This enabled the household kitchen to produce a great range of dishes all year round.

Tomatoes became increasingly popular at this time. Despite having been around for several centuries they had not been commonly used for culinary purposes, as their derivation from the nightshade family gave some cause for concern. The Victorians, with their penchant for growing under glass, popularised tomatoes more widely, and a skilled gardener could crop sequential varieties from June through to November. Varieties were grown with magnificent names such as Striped Stuffer, Bloody Butcher and Gardener's Delight, and in recent years the popularity of such heritage varieties has been gathering momentum again.

Despite a predominance of vegetables in the walled garden, however, they were not purely functional. Pergolas, tunnels and 'step-over' espaliers, which bordered pathways, were added over time in some gardens to provide a more pleasing aesthetic. Occasionally a walled garden was laid out to flowers alone, such as that at Winsford in Devon.

By Edwardian times, with the advent of the herbaceous planting style popularised by Gertrude Jekyll, more such borders had crept in to the walled garden. Yet much of the herbaceous planting seen in walled gardens today is relatively recent, taking the place of the original vegetable beds when reconstruction is done.

ABOVE LEFT This simple blackboard reveals the rotational plan at Attingham Park in Shropshire. RIGHT Today's gardeners at Knightshayes in Devon are once again producing numerous varieties of tomato, as did their forebears.

BORDERS AND BEDS

As with the use of the walls, the schemes adopted in walled kitchen gardens for the planting of the beds and borders were also based on some common conventions. The first was that the height of the wall should determine the depth of the border that ran beneath it. There were several reasons for this, but essentially it meant that not only would the border be in proportion to its backdrop, but the wall would also offer the most protection from the elements to its immediate border. Given that some of the greatest gardens were built during the eighteenth century, it is no surprise that the Georgian fascination with classical architectural proportion should also be felt in the layout of their kitchen gardens.

In the earliest gardens crops would be grown in raised or sunken beds to allow for irrigation channels. During the seventeenth century these levelled out into flat beds as the more delicate Mediterranean fruits and vegetables arrived. Artichokes, figs and grapes, for instance, all needed different types of microclimate and quantities of water.

LEFT The distinctive sloping beds at Trengwainton in Cornwall, cleverly designed to maximise space and capture sunlight while remaining well drained, overlooked by the head gardener's house.

BELOW LEFT The contemporary design that now fills the enormous walled area at Gordon Castle in Moray has allowed for wide, sweeping borders that flank the garden's central axis.

BELOW For many visitors, the crowded beds and borders of our sometimes more modest gardens, such as this one at Croft Castle, Herefordshire, conjure a real sense of being within an enchanted world.

THE FLOWER GARDEN

Flower and vegetable planting had become separated as kitchen gardens were banished to the further reaches of the estate during the eighteenth century, leaving the pleasure garden to focus upon more aesthetic floral and herbaceous displays. But by Victorian times flower-beds had become more integrated into the walled garden to satisfy the household's demand for cut flowers. Flower arranging was a required accomplishment of a young lady in Victorian times, so pressure on the gardeners to provide material was great. Flowers such as roses, tulips, peonies, carnations, chrysanthemums and dahlias were grown for this purpose, as was lavender for scented bags and other herbs for culinary and cosmetic use.

Providing flowers for the house, including buttonholes for the family and their guests, was an important part of the kitchen garden's role. The head gardener would have attended to much of this role himself, selecting, cutting and arranging flowers to ensure that a daily supply made its way to the house. He would also note every birthday, anniversary, dinner or other major event in the house calendar in his diary, so that the right flowers were in the right place at the right time. As wide herbaceous borders developed in the biggest gardens they might provide a ready source of flowers, but more usually a separate garden for the specific purpose was created, leaving the rest of the beds and borders undisturbed.

Dahlia 'Herbert Smith' growing in the walled garden at Wimpole Estate, Cambridgeshire.

PATHWAYS

Traditionally a path separated the borders from the central productive quarters, effectively framing the circuit of the walls. It also provided an essential route of access for the gardeners and their barrows, and would have been edged with a variety of materials including stone, brick and timber. The Victorians took this a stage further in the form of fired, rope-edged tiles, despite their fragility if kicked or knocked by a careless barrow or spade. By far the prettiest solution was to plant low box or yew hedging, reinstated today in many renovated gardens. Others have also invested in steel edging, to great aesthetic and practical effect.

LEFT The broad north–south pathway at Clumber Park in Nottinghamshire is central to the symmetry that this great garden enjoys across its subdivided 4 acres (1.6ha).

BELOW The frame yard at Llanerchaeron in west Wales is again the busy hub of the garden. Exploring it affords a behind-the-scenes peek at the workings of an intact eighteenth-century gem.

FRAME YARDS AND HOTBEDS

Since the late sixteenth century the idea of using the heat generated by decomposing horse manure and straw had gained in popularity. By the seventeenth century the hotbed had become an important tool in the growing of melons and cucumbers, as well as the nurturing of young plants through the colder months. Essentially a pile of steaming muck contained within a pit or wicker enclosure, the hotbed was topped with a wooden frame upon which glazed panels were mounted or simple cloches perched. These relatively temporary structures were unsightly and usually consigned to an area outside the garden walls. The frames which covered them eventually gave rise to the term 'frame yard' for the area in which they were situated. By the eighteenth century this had become an important and accepted part of the walled kitchen garden complex, and was often enclosed.

The successful use of the hotbed was fraught with difficulty. If the dung were too hot it might burn the plants that sat on top of it, and if too cold they would not grow; fumes were also feared to ruin the taste of crops. Nonetheless, in the hands of a skilled and patient gardener, the hotbed was invaluable – a factor that greatly hastened its development throughout the seventeenth and eighteenth centuries. The introduction of the glasshouse and the advent of the boiler and more controllable heating systems eventually replaced the once filthy hotbed, but its principles remained in the growing of exotic fruit and vegetables.

GLASSHOUSES

The most impressive and valued features in any walled kitchen garden were the numerous glass structures developed to house and grow an astonishing range of fruit and plants. From the moment the glasshouse was devised, its capacity to harness both heat and light, extending and accelerating the gardening year, ensured that it remained the subject of great architectural and scientific advancement.

Most glasshouses took advantage of the garden's walls and were built as lean-tos, although by the end of the nineteenth century many hot-house manufacturers offered full and three-quarter span examples. A well-appointed garden would boast a pinery, to produce pineapples, a vinery, to accommodate a grapevine, and possibly a separate peach house or peach cage. These might commonly share the south-facing range, divided with glazed internal walls and all heated through hot pipes fed from a solid fuel boiler on the other side of the wall.

Seeming to sink beneath a red sea of snapdragons, the restoration of the now-famous glasshouse range in the present-day Flower Garden at Heligan demonstrated how difficult and expensive such ambitious projects were when first undertaken during the early 1990s.

THE PINERY

The glass pinery was a development of the pineapple pit. Since the
late seventeenth century the pineapple had been a highly prized fruit;
the ability to produce them was a measure of a garden's capability.
Gardeners expert in growing them were highly valued, as was the
glasshouse or pinery where they were housed. The key ingredient in
producing pineapples was humid heat, ideally a steady 75°F (24°C),
which would mimic their native conditions in the West Indies. The
pinery would therefore have been heated – in its earliest incarnation
by hot walls or hotbeds filled with dung, but ultimately, in Victorian
times, with hot water pipes powered by a solid fuel boiler.

TANNER'S BARK

During the winter further heat was gained by setting individual
pineapple plants in pots within the pinery. They were set in a
deep mulch of tanner's bark, then readily available from the
thousands of tanneries in towns and villages across the country.
At the tannery, oak bark would have been added to huge vats
of water, in which leather hides were hung to colour or tan
them. Once a batch of bark had finished its useful contribution
to the process it was removed, but continued to ferment. This
latent heat was used in the pinery to great effect. Once its
purpose had been served at the end of the winter, the bark could
be composted. Tanner's bark is hard to come by today, but at
Tatton Park in Cheshire the gardeners use oak leaves, collected
during the autumn drop, to good effect.

THE VINERY

Grapes were a valued staple on the dinner tables of Britain's finest country houses. Dessert grapes were prized above all, remaining as popular with the Georgians as they had been with the Romans. With the advent of glass, dessert varieties, which depended upon indoor growing conditions, could be nurtured throughout the year – particularly during the crucial period between April and May, when the vines needed a steady 50°F (10°C) or more really to get going. The best gardens were expected to excel at both grape and pineapple production.

Ensuring that there were plenty of grapes during the winter required careful storage of selected bunches. An early method involved placing the stem of the bunch into clear empty bottles, which were then stacked on specially made angled shelves. Eventually, dedicated grape bottles with square sides and upturned necks were produced, allowing hundreds to be stored on normal shelves.

In addition to the main pinery–vinery range, a propagation house, tomato house and melon house – for cucumbers as well as melons – would have been essential for a large kitchen garden. As the nineteenth century wore on, an orchid house might also have been built, if the owner had an eye for them. The Victorian passion for exploration encouraged intrepid plant hunters to seek out new species of plants from the farthest reaches of the empire – a risky but lucrative business. At Tatton Park in Cheshire, Paxton's fabulous fernery took the idea of the glasshouse one stage further. His towering iron structure housed a veritable equatorial world, the estate's pride and joy.

The glasshouse that began in the eighteenth century had been transformed by the early twentieth. From a simple building that harnessed the heat of the sun, or was supplemented with hot walls, it had become a sophisticated architectural delight. In an age before computers, glasshouse design had mastered the management of heat, light and air flow to create a highly controlled environment, able to produce the finest fruit and flowers all year round.

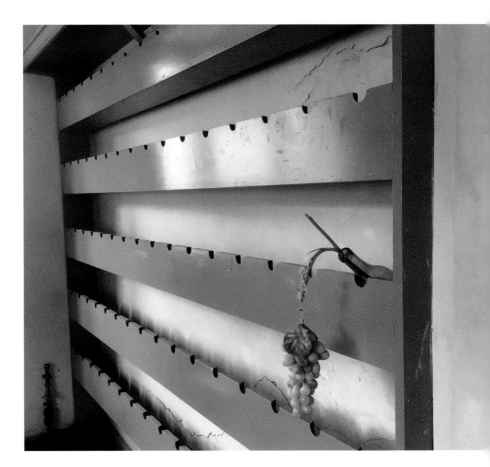

Most grapes grown were dessert varieties. So prized were they at Tyntesfield in Somerset that their storage rack was built inside the head gardener's office, safely under lock and key, from where he could also look out upon the garden's splendid late-Victorian orangery (above right).

ORANGERIES

From the hotbed to the hot wall, and the careful cajoling of fruit trees and other crops, walled gardeners of the past developed ingenious ways to extend the productive year. Yet by the eighteenth century rapid advances in the manufacture of glass and its use in construction transformed the fortunes of the walled garden, dramatically increasing its potential for producing exotic fruit and plants from across a growing empire.

The properties of glass had been established during the previous century, when Dutch growers recognised its value in the overwintering of citrus trees. Open-sided buildings with tiled roofs were enclosed during the winter with glazed screens, which protected orange and lemon trees from frost and wind while allowing in light. The trees were grown in wooden planters, enabling them to be moved inside and out as the season dictated. These 'orangeries' were given impetus in Britain when William of Orange and his wife Mary came to the throne in 1689. Dutch experts installed an orangery at Hampton Court Palace, inspiring the nobility to follow suit on their own grounds.

The orangery emerged as a distinct architectural component through the eighteenth and nineteenth centuries. It morphed in some degree into the Victorian conservatory, a space for the conserving of plants over the winter. As the eighteenth-century landscape movement reshaped many estates, the orangery concept combined with the fashion for building temples and other follies across an improved landscape. Examples include James Paine's Temple of Diana at Weston Park in Shropshire, laid out by 'Capability' Brown, and the Temple Greenhouse at Croome Park in Worcestershire, designed by Robert Adam.

HEAD GARDENER'S HOUSE

The head gardener of a large estate would have been among the most literate members of staff. Adept at keeping records and managing the workforce across all the gardens, his house was a significant perk of the job. It would have been well appointed, and was usually located either within or adjacent to the walled garden. The head gardener was an expert in every area of garden production. He would have been keen to have a house and, importantly, an office that allowed him to look out on one of the estate's most prized assets – the kitchen garden and its precious glasshouses.

Given the obvious social and economic gulf between the aristocracy and their employees, it is easy to imagine a deferential world in which the gardeners and their efforts may have been underappreciated. Yet while there was always a clear and concise pecking order, in gardens which remained focused on horticultural endeavour, for example those built by the Egertons at Tatton Park in Cheshire, I'd like to think the relationship between the head gardener and his employer was as cordial as it was professional. Both parties were determined to grow the best produce possible, albeit for slightly different reasons.

The handsome facade of the head gardener's house at Clumber Park in Nottinghamshire lacks a front door. Important and valued as he may have been, he and his family still had to use a side, or tradesman's, entrance.

BACK SHEDS AND OTHER OUTBUILDINGS

Gardening on an industrial scale creates a lot of mess, something quite at odds with the clean and orderly world of the walled garden. As we have seen, the slips that surrounded most large gardens were also useful productive spaces, particularly those to the south, west and east. This left the northern slips, the area behind the garden's south-facing wall, as the obvious place to store equipment, produce and the usual muck and bits and pieces that we might expect in a busy garden. In the cool shade a range of buildings and bays sprang up, making good use of an otherwise largely unproductive area. They were also ideally placed to accommodate the later ancillary equipment required by the south-facing glasshouses, built against the other side of the wall.

These lean-tos and other outbuildings, known as the back sheds, were one of the most important and useful parts of a busy kitchen garden. The earliest examples were little more than simple open structures for carts and tools. In gardens with hot walls they provided cover for the fire pits and the fuel these required. Over time these open cart bays in older gardens were filled in, for example those at Llanerchaeron in west Wales. Some new spaces were used for gardeners' bothies, simple accommodation for the most junior staff. Others became tool stores, potting sheds or fruit and root stores. As the walled garden developed, by the end of the nineteenth century the back sheds were purpose-

built ranges containing boiler rooms, which heated the glasshouses through a series of hot water pipes, bothies and a host of storage areas. At Knightshayes in Devon the state-of-the-art back sheds included a rare mushroom house, complete with slate-lined shelving to contain the beds within their darkened room, as well as numerous storage areas and garden offices. At nearby Tyntesfield in Somerset the back sheds were redesigned with a beautiful late Victorian classical facade, creating a stunning backdrop to the flower garden, frame yard, orangery and extensive galvanised glasshouses that they overlooked.

ABOVE The uniquely terraced layout at Knightshayes in Devon provided a large utility area to the rear of the main garden, containing bothies, stores and boiler rooms, and the upper frame yard. The head gardener's house is just beyond, well placed to observe the garden by both day and night.

LEFT This aerial shot of Tyntesfield in Somerset allows a fine view of the garden, the frame yard with its extensive range of galvanised glasshouses and classical back sheds, and some of the ancillary cottages that the estate's senior staff would have used. The head gardener's house is to the left of the orangery.

ABOVE Head gardeners had to be literate, expert, and highly organised, skills many would have learned in various gardens before gaining a top job. Seed cabinets like this one at Calke Abbey in Derbyshire were an essential feature of the head gardener's domain.

WATER

The central feature of the traditional walled kitchen garden was perhaps its most useful. The provision of a ready source of water is vital to the success of any garden, particularly a productive one. The dipping pond was either a well or an outlet fed by underground pipes from a nearby lake or other source, ensuring that the gardeners had easy access to as much water as required. These days, of course, most renovated walled kitchen gardens have a network of underground pipes connecting taps in almost every bed, but the original kitchen gardens enjoyed no such luxury. The dipping pond allowed buckets and cans to be filled quickly, while large galvanised water carriers helped to transport larger quantities to more distant beds and borders.

The central pond at Coughton Court in Warwickshire remains a striking focal point at the heart of this now ornamental garden.

BEES

Bees were an important asset in a busy kitchen garden – not only as a source of honey, but also as hard-working pollinators, flitting between plants and flowers. Not all walled gardens had their own hives, but several larger ones did. Attingham Park in Shropshire has a very elegant bee house designed by Humphry Repton. Both Heligan in Cornwall and Packwood House in Warwickshire have preserved examples of bee boles, brick niches into which straw hives or skeps could be stood, sheltered from the worst of the weather.

LEFT These bee boles at Packwood House in Warwickshire kept out the worst of the weather very effectively.

ABOVE Hives such as these at Knightshayes Court in Devon are a common sight in many revived kitchen gardens across the country, adding interest, honey and a willing army of pollinators.

FANTASY AND REALITY

To walk through our fantasy garden would be a treat, but in many respects nowhere near as rewarding as discovering the reality of the many surviving gardens now open to the public. In exploring these wondrous places, we are stepping into a world that would once have been open to only a few. Fortunately today many are open to the public for all to enjoy. Thanks to those who have brought some of the finest examples back into use, we can appreciate the unique atmosphere of a productive walled garden bursting with life.

If our fantasy garden did exist, some might say there would be no need to visit any other, and that would be a tragedy. For in visiting the gardens that follow I have discovered an immersive, addictive blend of architectural, horticultural and social history. Walled gardens are all the richer because they are so individually distinct and all, when you know what to look for, have a fascinating story to reveal.

RIGHT An inviting archway provides a tantalizing glimpse of what lies beyond in the extensive walled gardens at Felbrigg in Norfolk.

PAGES 86–87 When viewing from ground level, it can be difficult to appreciate the scale of some of our biggest walled gardens, as here at Gordon Castle in Moray.

PART TWO

EXPLORING WALLED GARDENS

3

Early walled gardens

The riotous catmint that fills the long border at
Easton Walled Gardens in Lincolnshire softens
the hard landscaping of the boundary walls.

Early walled gardens are hard to find, but the enclosure at Easton in Lincolnshire gives a sense of their scale and size, despite these later towers.

Enclosed gardens may be traced at least as far back as Roman times. Yet one of the great challenges in understanding their development is the scarcity of very early examples. Walled gardens of the past were productive and industrious places, often redeveloped or relocated as horticultural ideas changed and family fortunes fluctuated. These utilitarian areas had to keep up with new ideas, tastes and the demands of a growing estate and its population.

In its earliest and purest form, a walled garden was a modest, functional space. If it needed improving or expanding and the resources were available, then so be it. Recognisably early examples of walled kitchen gardens are thus rare today, having been either built over or knocked down and relocated to a more distant but improved location. So what might the walled garden of the fifteenth or sixteenth century have looked like, and how did it originate?

One of the most notable of early garden writers, Thomas Hill, published a surprisingly practical gardening guide, *The Gardener's Labyrinth*, in 1577. Among the sound advice it contained were smatterings of astrology and the supernatural, but it's easy to see why it was a hit, being reprinted several times. Hill's book not only describes the best ways to manage soil and maximise output, but also gives details on the layout and dimensions of beds to aid their watering. With extensive quotes from classical authors such as Cato and Pliny, it is clear that Hill and writers like him were drawing upon long-established ancient works on gardening which, by his time, were at least a thousand years old. These in turn must have informed the layout of earlier monastic gardens, within whose literate communities

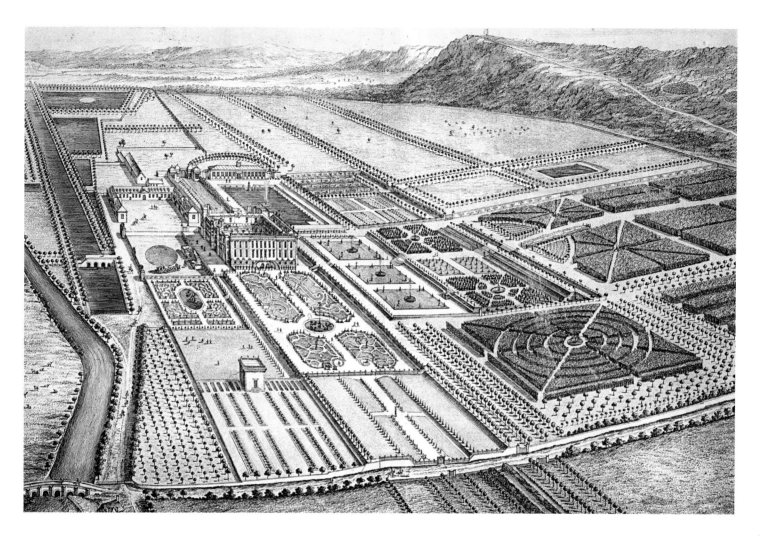

these texts were assiduously copied and preserved over many centuries, right across Europe. Within their cloistered enclosures many in holy orders were expert in the cultivation of herbs for medicinal uses, along with fruit, vegetables and even vines.

We may draw upon all these sources to describe the walled gardens of the Elizabethan age. Place of order and beauty, they were modest in size and located near to, if not alongside, the houses they served. The kitchen garden was but one horticultural element; other areas, perhaps including a formal flower garden, were formally laid out with symmetry and colour. Divided into quadrants, themselves bordered by box hedges or similar, the late medieval walled garden was already established as a place of intensive production, but of course without later features such as glasshouses and hot walls. These early examples, with no glasshouses or hot walls, represented the essence of walled kitchen gardening in its purest form.

Chatsworth House, Derbyshire, c1700. The house still overlooks gardens and orchards, yet by the end of the century most estates moved their kitchen gardens into the park, often screening them with pleasure grounds.

91

BLICKLING ESTATE
Norfolk

The Blickling Estate in North Norfolk is a rare survivor, and not simply because the house itself has remained largely untouched since it was rebuilt in the early seventeenth century. The magnificent facade that greets the visitor today surrounds a much earlier fourteenth-century property, Dagworth Manor. Its history is remarkable, not least as the former family seat of Sir Thomas Boleyn, whose daughter Anne's marriage to Henry VIII helped to change the course of English history. In the 1940s Blickling's rich story took another twist when it became one of the first and most complete donations to the National Trust under the Country Houses Scheme. The Estate's then owner, Lord Lothian, helped to establish the Trust's new direction for the rest of the twentieth century. The principle of donation in lieu of death duties was born and backed up by his unprecedented gift to the nation.

In the post-war years, Blickling's walled garden, like many others, fell into disuse. Covering some 4 acres (1.6ha), it was clearly once capable of supporting a house the size of which we see today, and is of interest for several reasons. First, it is the most recent to have been restored by the National Trust over a very focused five-year project. Second, although it has clearly been expanded during its life, it almost certainly started out as a much smaller affair, possibly as far back as the fourteenth century. Thirdly, its development is so closely allied to the fortunes of the house that we can use the well-documented history of Blickling's ownership to chart the development, in broad stages, of its walled garden, from Tudor times to the present day.

Enormous efforts were made to reinstate the walled garden. On my visit, just 18 months into the project, I arrived unsure of how much there would be to see. But head gardener Paul Underwood and project manager Mike Owers showed me a breathtaking array of colour and produce. In just a few short months, the lawns had been replaced with a thriving garden that looked as if it had been established for years. For Mike, who trained there a decade ago, the chance to lead the regeneration was a dream come true. 'When I first came here, I remember mowing this lot with a tractor, imagining what it must have been like in its heyday. I knew then that if the opportunity arose to reinstate even a part of it, I wanted to be involved.'

Over several years Mike and Paul, who shared his passion for walled gardens, made the case for investing in Blickling's garden. Both were clear about the aims. 'We could not realistically have transformed all four acres,' explained Paul. 'So we

RIGHT The recent transformation of the kitchen garden at Blickling has been both rapid and dramatic, with fantastic results. This south-facing border would once have supported a range of glasshouses, but today it is instead a riot of colour.

PAGES 94–95 In its heyday, Blickling's walled gardens covered 4 acres (1.6ha). By reconstructing just 1 acre (0.4ha), its modern gardeners have created a beautiful, productive garden that is focused on providing for the needs of the house today.

focused on one acre in the north-western corner. As a result it's not a renovation, it's a regeneration. In other words, we have reinstated a garden that fulfils the needs of the house today, rather than trying to recreate a pastiche from the past.'

The results are stunning. By limiting the project to this 1 acre (0.4ha) quadrant, they have been able to base the new garden around its original key components. Although some have been lost, including most of its former glasshouses, they have renovated those that have survived, namely the propagation house and melon house. Both are now full of produce.

They have also brought the bothy back into use as a tool shed and base for the army of dedicated volunteers who have helped to make this ambitious transformation a reality, and in record time. The planting areas, laid out in a traditional way, include a herb garden, cut flower borders, rotational vegetable plots, a huge soft fruit area and raised beds. Crisp steel edging now surrounds the cultivated area, along with both espaliered fruit trees and cordons trained onto new iron and wire supports. The fruit trees here are mainly East Anglian varieties, although the team has reintroduced several varieties, such as Gravenstein, Warner's King and American Mother, that they know were grown in the garden in the late eighteenth century by its head gardener, H. G. Oclee.

A recently compiled historic report helps make sense of the garden's development through a series of old plans and photos and led to an unexpected and exciting reappraisal of how it may have evolved. The front of the great house is flanked by two huge ranges of ancillary buildings, with the original walled garden almost certainly established

ABOVE RIGHT The key to maintaining interest in any garden is the cultivation of the next generation of gardeners. Here they are encouraged by this neat row of miniature wheelbarrows and watering cans.

OPPOSITE A recent study of both the walls and the brick coping that runs along the top of them has helped to determine how different styles relate to different phases of construction.

LEFT This redundant tap on the heating pipes in one of the glasshouses has been left stuck in the past, perhaps recording the moment decades ago that it was turned for the last time.

ABOVE Unusually, Blickling's gardeners have used both gravel and grass pathways in their layout. They are also adding a series of iron hoops that will eventually support trained fruit trees along its central axis.

behind the western range. It was a much smaller enclosure compared to all that survives today, clearly too small to service the present house.

This smaller walled enclosure is unusual because it is located close to the original house and has not been moved: this part of Blickling never underwent a landscape makeover of the sort favoured by 'Capability' Brown or Humphry Repton. Although lavishly rebuilt at the start of the seventeenth century into the house we see today, subsequent owners sought not to reinvent Blickling, unlike many other earlier country seats. The result is that while the house was improved and embellished, its walled garden was simply expanded. The great walls that surround the northern half were probably added around the 1740s, as suggested from a bill of sale for the land required; later improvements included the addition of glasshouses.

Eventually it would have boasted a peach house, pinery and vinery, all now sadly gone, along its south-facing wall, as well as attendant bothies and boiler rooms attached to the walls outside. Cold frames and a fruit store were built in the south-western corner and quadrant. It is also unusual that the line of the great walls follows at its western and southern sides the line of the village road. The likes of 'Capability' Brown would simply have erased or re-routed it, but not here. The garden's layout has preserved a glimpse into its evolution, while today in large part reflecting its late Victorian arrangements.

The story of Blickling covers nearly 600 years, although there is little left of the Tudor garden. It is humbling to think that this slice of Norfolk has been gardened for so long. If Anne Boleyn's ghost is still here, it may well be accompanied by those of many old gardeners, watching the regeneration with interest.

The restored propagation house is a perfect example of a three-quarter span glasshouse, partially sunk into the ground below. Based upon a shorter rear supporting wall that would not allow for a traditional lean-to arrangement, three-quarter designs maximised light from their south-facing aspect while providing additional height, space and light within.

When it comes to walls it is often assumed that all you can see was built at the same time, especially with no detailed history of construction. This may well be true of later Victorian kitchen gardens such as at Knightshayes, but it is rarely the case for gardens that began in the late seventeenth or eighteenth centuries, and have been much altered since.

Understanding how walls and other structures relate to one another is an essential tool for working out the order in which features were added or demolished. Fortunately much of what we have to decipher is brick-built, which makes calculating a chronological sequence easier. Identifying distinct phases of construction and piecing them together into a historic narrative can reveal much about how a garden was used and developed, even if we cannot tie a particular element to a specific month or year.

Central to this idea is the nature of brickwork itself. Bricks are laid in courses, variously offset one above the other and bedded together with lime mortar, and different styles combine distinct orders of both headers and stretchers. Recognising these styles and noting where they appear in a complex of walls may reveal a specific moment of construction – the stylistic signature of a builder or designer.

These stylistic clues are also useful when looking at a wall's copings, the materials and styles used to make the top watertight, without which the wall may collapse in just a few years. Copings can take many forms, including simple stones set upright, worked stone slabs, a course of brick headers and tiles or specially fired bricks created for a particular

LEFT Recognising different phases of construction is greatly helped in gardens built from brick. Here at Felbrigg in Norfolk, the main garden wall on the right is earlier than that which joins it to the left, as revealed in the uneven brick courses and crude jointing.

wall. Where the coping has a distinct design, it usually follows that every wall built at the same time should look the same. However, there are plenty of examples where the original may have been removed, or a poor copy made to help things blend in. Close scrutiny is thus essential, as is the ability to put yourself in the builder's mind. Are you are looking at the work of the estates' master mason, or a cheap practical fix by an unskilled bricklayer?

One key area to study is the point where walls meet. This might be where a main wall is connected to a dividing element or where a building is attached to the wall that it shares. In general buildings and other structures that are planned to be built together are bonded together, their bricks carefully interlocked like cogs. Where something has been added later, this tends not to be the case and the addition is readily apparent. Not only are the bricks not 'toothed' into their adjacent wall, but the coursing or lines of bricks may also be out of alignment. Spotting walls and buildings that have clearly been added on is particularly useful when trying to phase and date bothies, boiler houses or other elements in a garden complex.

ABOVE The lime-washed brickwork and arched dwarf wall show this to be the remains of the inside of the vinery at Blickling Hall in Norfolk. Accurately dating such an addition or demolition requires detailed research of plans, maps and documentary evidence – and often good old-fashioned intuition.

101

EASTON WALLED GARDENS
Lincolnshire

'A dream of Nirvana – the whole place is almost too good to be true.'
Franklin D. Roosevelt

Not every garden has the privilege of being celebrated by a future leader of the free world, but that is exactly what befell the gardens and once beautiful house of Easton. Roosevelt made the comments after his third and final visit to Easton in 1905, aged 23 and caught up in the romance of his honeymoon. To him the gardens and house must have seemed the epitome of the classic English country retreat, elegantly spread over a captivating river valley in rural Lincolnshire. No one could have foreseen that less than 50 years later the house he so enjoyed would have been demolished and its ancient gardens abandoned to decades of neglect and decay.

The garden of Easton might have remained lost but for the determination of Lady Ursula Cholmeley, whose husband's family have owned the site and surrounding farmland since 1592. In 2001 Ursula, herself newly married, started to explore the overgrowth and ruins – all that remained of the great house and garden. The once grand and

LEFT The remaining glasshouses at Easton simmer in the summer sun, while flowers enjoy the cooler air outside.
RIGHT Drones now give us the opportunity to get a bird's-eye view of many walled kitchen gardens. Here the busy contemporary kitchen garden contrasts with the simplicity of the original garden beyond, today planted with fruit trees and dominated by the yew avenue.

opulent hall had been so damaged through use by the Parachute Regiment in the Second World War that it was no longer worth keeping; the house was pulled down in 1951. The garden, whose walls stretched out beneath it across the valley below, had all but disappeared. It was in a state of near ruin, while the later Victorian outbuildings were in complete collapse. Yet records and pictures remained, and these have helped to create a bold reimagining of the gardens, set against the scant ruins and traces of the former family home.

The house shown in photographs from the nineteenth century is a far cry from its predecessor. When the Cholmeleys first acquired the estate at the end of the sixteenth century, the conveyance noted orchards, meadows and gardens, helping to identify Easton as a rare example of an early walled garden. We can only imagine the appearance of the first house, replaced by a sprawling Victorian mansion, but the simple walled garden, originally created in the late sixteenth century, is Easton's crowning glory today.

The walled garden is situated opposite the remains of the house on the far side of the River Witham. Given its aspect on the opposing east-facing slope of this modest valley, the house was afforded a view into the walled enclosure as it developed over four centuries in a way that many others were not. The walls themselves are not high, and were never raised to accommodate glasshouses or other outbuildings. They have remained largely as they were built: a simple barrier around a garden in a landscape itself left

OPPOSITE Once lost in the undergrowth and in danger of total collapse, the restored neoclassical bridge remains an iconic architectural centrepiece.

BELOW Wildflower meadows cascade down the terraced banks that once underlined the base of the mansion, whilst yew cones guard the steps that led up to the terrace.

largely untouched, despite centuries of changing trends and tastes that have altered other historic estates.

The garden was separated from the house by an ornamental garden, terraced down the slope towards an elegant neoclassical bridge that is the garden's most iconic feature. The mixed border beyond, some 262ft (80m) in length, is divided by a central entrance into an enormous, yew-lined walk that now splits the walled garden into two.

The regenerative planting has not sought to replicate past endeavours. Ursula Cholmeley had long planned to create informal planting schemes within a formal structure, which is exactly what she has achieved. The walled garden is not tied to production apart from the fruit trees it now boasts and rose gardens set within wildflower meadows. It is still flanked by its ancient towers, their facades perhaps embellished as later Victorian or Edwardian follies, from a time when the house and garden's future seemed assured.

One important question to ask is how did this early walled enclosure survive at all? Over the centuries it might have been extended and

OPPOSITE The restored glass-house shelters a colourful bed of tulips. Beyond is the former boiler house and bothy that served the peach house, the ornate remains of which can be seen on the wall above.

BELOW LEFT The west front of Easton Hall in 1890, with its immaculate terrace overlooked by the peach house to the left and the mansion to the right. Such photographic clues, while often rare, are invaluable in tracing a garden's history.

developed out of all recognition, like many others, or demolished to accommodate new horticultural and architectural trends.

The answer may have more to do with the family's fortunes than a curatorial vision; the Cholmeleys never really had the resources that constant redevelopment would require. 'Capability' Brown would have been beyond their means, as would the costs of relocating the walled garden. Not only were such ideas unaffordable, they were also unnecessary; everything worked well just where and how it was. In truth, Easton's circumstances probably reflect those of the majority of kitchen gardens across the country. Not much was added until the rebuilding of the house in the early nineteenth century, and the work then took place towards the house, not within the existing walls of the sixteenth-century original garden. The peach house was a useful addition, as were the buildings that serviced it. These look out eastward to the modern 'pickery', a richly planted wildflower garden created by Ursula Cholmeley.

The pickery and its neighbouring glasshouses provide a classic walled-garden ambience that is both practical and fitting. The vegetable patch, flower garden and greenhouses date to the Edwardian era; they have required much restoration but now work hard to supply the café and shop. Easton is a garden the family love and of whose regeneration they are rightly proud. Rescued from ruin and neglect, it both reflects the past and looks confidently to the future.

The 'pickery' is Ursula Cholmeley's pride and joy, and is a vibrant part of her own interpretation of a working kitchen garden, which now supplies Easton's popular café.

4 Gardens of the revolution: the eighteenth century

Perhaps one of the most famous kitchen garden doorways in the country, it's thought this one at Attingham Park in Shropshire was a later addition, put in by the great Humphry Repton.

The eighteenth century was for Britain an unrivalled period of global expansion, invention and investment. Money and military might consolidated trading links and territorial gains in the East and West Indies, while developments in science and technology fostered industrial expansion on an unprecedented scale. Consumerism flourished both at home and in colonies abroad, as a newly urban population revelled in its obsessions with tea, china, fashions and display. In this confident society, unafraid to challenge its past, the humble walled garden enjoyed perhaps its most formative period. Many grand houses and their parklands were remodelled in the favoured Georgian neoclassical style, while new estates reflected the social ambitions of an affluent commercial class who sought to emulate the aristocracy in creating fitting family seats.

Alongside all these changes there ran another revolution of a very different kind, whose effects were seen and encouraged only by the privileged few. It was led by architect and landscape designer William Kent, widely regarded as the father of the English Landscape Movement. From the 1740s Kent, and later Lancelot 'Capability' Brown, among others, led a transformation of the British country house which often had a profound effect on the development of the walled garden. Champions of a more naturalistic setting for these great mansions, this new class of landscape gardener redesigned both parkland and house to create an often idyllic classical setting that focused on eye-lines, vanishing points, and carefully composed views that demanded no unnecessary interruption. As a result,

anything that distracted from the often remodelled house was erased from the composition. The result was that many walled gardens were either redesigned to fit the scheme or simply demolished and relocated far from the house they had originally served, tucked away behind swathes of trees and pleasure grounds. In these instances, it also provided an opportunity to site them close to stableyards and their ready source of manure, and provide the garden with a better site that captured the best of the sun and provided for improved drainage.

The new fashion for pineapples and other tropical fruits proved a catalyst for technological innovation. Dutch horticulturalists had established a reputation for quality and invention, pioneering heated glasshouses, or stove houses as they became known, in Holland. By the early eighteenth century the stove house, using either fermenting dung or direct heat through underfloor flues, had been adopted in Britain. Heating processes using flues, pans of hot charcoal or tanner's bark, another Dutch idea (p.74), could maintain temperatures within the glasshouse through the coldest of winters; indeed, all were provided with windows to release excess heat.

As the century developed, so did techniques for manufacturing glass and glasshouses. Their position relative to the sun became a more exact science, and gradually fruits from all over the world were cultivated and propagated in Britain from imported plants and seeds.

The late eighteenth-century walled gardens at Llanerchaeron, west Wales, are overlooked by successive generations of glasshouses and the head gardener's house.

ATTINGHAM PARK
Shropshire

'Coming in here is like entering an oasis, an oasis of calm against the troubles of the world outside.'
Katherine Dowd, Senior Gardener

The walled garden at Attingham Park has played an important role in developing my fascination with these spaces. I first came here in 2010, when its restoration was gathering pace. Today the garden is bursting with life and produce, its key features and buildings beautifully restored.

Built in the 1780s, the walled garden was probably established at the same time that Noel Hill, 1st Lord Berwick, commissioned the Scottish architect George Steuart to build Attingham Hall and stables; these still remain as a rare example of his work. Hill's political support for William Pitt the Younger was rewarded with a peerage and endowments that enabled him to spare no expense in creating a family seat befitting a well-connected and rising member of the aristocracy.

In accordance with convention, the walled garden was built some distance from the main house, in this case to the north, although as close to the stables and their supply of manure as was possible. The gardens were probably invisible from the house, concealed by well-established pleasure grounds ringed with a ha-ha. The 2nd Lord Berwick's accession, following his father's death aged only 44, left the house unfurnished and unfinished. In 1805 John Nash was brought in to complete the project; he may well have also influenced the walled garden design, as he did at Llanerchaeron in west Wales (p.124). The walled garden covers 2 acres (0.8ha) and is set within warm red brick walls, 12ft (3.7m) in height, almost certainly mined from clay pits on the estate. The brief walk from the stableyard (now a café) through the pleasure grounds of mature trees brings a tantalizing glimpse of the long southern wall with its curved corners and a single, inviting doorway.

On my second visit, it was clear that Attingham's former senior gardener, Kate Nicoll, her successor Katherine Dowd and an army of volunteers had been busy. What was once a derelict, overgrown and forlorn eyesore has now been transformed into

LEFT This colourful contemporary plan of Attingham's walled garden clearly shows the irregularity of its shape and the extent of both the main garden and the frame yard to the east.

RIGHT The restored pinery and vinery that dominate the frame yard are just part of the huge glasshouse complex, built in 1924. Such investment was doubtless needed to replace earlier examples that had gone beyond economical repair.

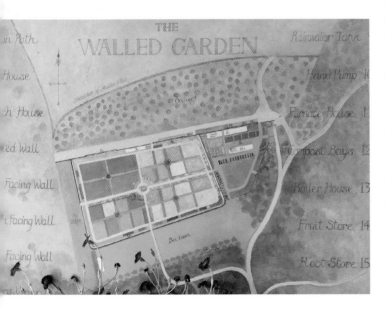

RIGHT The walled garden at Attingham, as well as supplying its café with produce, also contains cut flowers for the house.

FAR RIGHT The central walk and border looking east towards the frame yard is once again flanked with iron estate railings painted in 'Attingham grey', supporting espaliered fruit trees. Evidence for them came from the chance find of an early photograph, which set in motion their reinstatement.

a model of beauty and productivity. Divided into classic quadrants and sub-quadrants, three-quarters of the available space is now under cultivation, rotated every six years, and is supplying the café at Attingham. Kate, who drove the restoration plan forward from its tentative start back in 2008, is clear about its popularity with visitors, two-thirds of whom come for the gardens and park alone. She describes it as 'an attraction with purpose', able to provide food and cut flowers for the estate. As Kate explains: 'Our continued efforts to bring it back to life aren't a pastiche of life gone by; they've created a living, breathing place that our visitors really appreciate.'

What makes Attingham so captivating is that all its key elements, except the peach house, have survived and been brought back into everyday use. Adjacent to the garden at the eastern end is a door that leads into the slightly later walls of the frame yard, in which the ambition of the estate's former gardeners is clear to see. With a pineapple house,

neighbouring vinery and separate melon and tomato houses, along with the bothy and cold frames, the whole is set beautifully within recently revived cut flower-beds that are a riot of colour. Traditionally it would have been the senior gardener's job to cut and prepare flowers for the house and so it remains today, ably supported by skilled volunteers.

Behind the great south-facing wall are the essential ancillary buildings that such a garden required, and which were continually developed over time. The back sheds at Attingham comprise tool stores, a mushroom store, various cart barns and later boiler houses. However of real note is their root store, a subterranean world in which all the root vegetables were kept once harvested. Timber hatches at ground level covered chutes that enabled barrows of produce, such as carrots, potatoes or parsnips, to be poured into brick-built pits below. Around 35 cu. ft (1 cu. m) in size, each pit was filled with sand covering successive layers of stock. The cold and dark conditions meant that in some cases

OPPOSITE ABOVE Attingham's back sheds stand behind the frame yard, and are a fine example of how what were once little more than open cart bays in many gardens evolved. Here they included a tool and potting shed, both a boiler and mushroom house, and access to an underground root store (p.123).

OPPOSITE BELOW The frame yard is a superb example of how these vital spaces were accommodated in the biggest gardens. Here it was enclosed in what appears to be a later wall, which aside from a huge range of glasshouses, also encompasses the recently replanted flower garden and gardener's bothy.

vegetables could last for almost a year, as gardeners at Attingham have proved. Such simple and innovative storage solutions made the walled garden an annual year-round provider to many a great estate. However, it was in producing the exotic, such as pineapples and melons, that most sought to excel, and Attingham's owners and gardeners were no exception.

Opposite the main entrance doorway, possibly installed by Humphry Repton during his later remodelling of the park, are the foundations of the peach house. Repton may have designed this too, creating a classic focal point for anyone entering the garden. When first built, a wall of glittering glass would have welcomed the visitor, while walls behind were heated with a traditional system of internal flues. Interestingly, archaeological evidence suggests that many of Attingham's flues, which pepper the length of the south-facing northern wall, were not used for long. This might point to an original garden without glasshouses relying on heated flues, abandoned when glass features were added later.

Attingham's layout is also worthy of note. Today it has been replanted in a classic series of quadrants, but this revealed that, despite appearances, the oblong enclosure is not completely true. Both the eastern and southern walls are shorter than their opposites, creating something of a trapezoidal shape. This subtly allowed more valuable planting space

on the all-important and heated south-facing wall, while also ensuring that the western boundary caught the last rays of the setting sun. Somewhat off-centre is a dipping pool which, if aerial photos are to be believed, may also have been linked to another oval pool in the eastern portion. This has yet to be found, but future investigation of this shady buried feature will prove interesting.

Based upon early photographs, the main pathways are today flanked with reconstructed high estate railings, providing more space on which to grow a wide range of espaliered pears and apples. The main east–west axis, which connects the garden to the frame yard, is supplemented with wide herbaceous borders that attempt to replicate the scented and colourful promenade the Berwicks, their guests and gardeners might have enjoyed.

The fortunes of Attingham's walled garden changed in the later twentieth century, as the garden became first a football pitch and then a Christmas tree plantation in the 1990s. The National Trust took the decision to restore it in 2008, with a dedicated team of staff and volunteers whose passion is obvious. For Katherine, whose horticultural apprenticeship has been built upon the garden's transformation, it has a charm all of its own. She describes it as 'a world within a world', where you can feel connected to generations of past gardeners who cared for the same unique space.

OPPOSITE Kitchen gardens lend themselves to a good sense of fun. This scarecrow at Attingham is clearly earning its keep.

As with many walled gardens, at Attingham precious little information survives to tell us how and when each component was installed or developed. To Kate and Katherine this has been both frustrating and surprising, given that head gardeners would have been among the most literate members of the estate team. Assiduous record keeping year after year focused on what was planted where and when, and on prevailing weather conditions and results – yet, excepting sundries such as seeds and tools, there are few notes of additional equipment being installed or buildings constructed. This could be because items of major expense were managed by the wider estate's land agents and its owners, falling outside the province of the head gardener. Despite the near bankruptcy of the 2nd Earl Berwick in 1827, which resulted in many of Attingham Hall's contents being sold off, investment in the garden clearly continued. Glasshouses and the water heating system were all provided over successive phases; even in 1924 the frame yard and its various houses were overhauled once again, at a time when many gardens began to decline.

However, the Attingham archive does hold one rare and important set of records. The 1908 log book of head gardener John Atkinson, only recently discovered, has provided a revealing insight into the garden's management. A century later, Kate and her team decided to replicate his entries for the nineteenth of each month over a five-year period that covered much of the restoration. What started out as a commemorative exercise, comparing the weather, planting schemes and produce gained, has now produced a fascinating comparison of the gardening year. The archives have also revealed the name of the first female walled gardener at Attingham. Mary Gatecliffe worked there throughout the Second World War, producing much-needed wartime supplies.

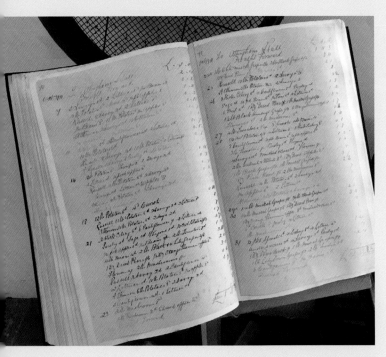

LEFT The head gardener's log book, a rare find from 1908, allows us to see a detailed comparison of planting schemes and weather patterns a century ago.

ROOT STORES

For a successful kitchen garden seeking to supply food all year round, storing produce was as important as producing it. The challenges of making food last required the walled kitchen gardener to be both inventive and cunning.

The storing of fruit required specific methods; so did the storage of root crops such as parsnips, potatoes, beets and carrots. Attingham Park's example of a root store is typical of some of the better ones. Gardeners of the past required stores that allowed their conditions to be controlled, particularly in respect of temperature and light. The root store was often built as a subterranean vault underneath the fruit store, where it was easier to spot signs that rats or rot might be damaging the winter's supply. At Attingham the store is built in the shaded row of the back sheds, below ground level; it was divided on one side into troughs or boxes of about 10¾ sq. ft (1 sq. m). Above each, a small hatch at ground level allowed crops to be gently tipped into their respective trough. As with fruit, the careful handling of crops to avoid unnecessary damage and bruising was key to a good storage system. Successive layers of crops were laid out in their troughs, then covered with sand until each was full. The free-draining sand helped to mitigate any damp issues, while the tunnel or vault itself was carefully corbelled to prevent water getting in.

Surface clamping could also be used in the absence of an underground option. Instead of sand, crops such as potatoes were piled up in successive layers of straw and then finally one of soil. This effectively insulated them from the elements, yet allowed them to breathe and sweat without rotting. This was a riskier proposition because rain and pests were more likely to get in, but could nonetheless prove successful. Meanwhile, the vaulted store might also be used for the transplanting and partial burial of certain salad crops, such as lettuce and chicory, which would have retained their roots for the purpose. These simple techniques, developed over many years, allowed the walled garden to provide a rich array of ingredients through winter into early spring. There was indeed a cost to this, often involving the building of some expensive and elaborate structures. Yet investment to generate produce from the walled garden was usually deemed worthwhile, impressing those who dined with the nation's rich and powerful.

BELOW LEFT Root crops are once again a staple in many kitchen gardens.

BELOW The root store at Attingham Park is still used, and is as successful today as it undoubtedly always was.

123

LLANERCHAERON
Ceredigion

Tucked away in the beautiful Aeron valley lies one of my favourite National Trust properties. Described as a Regency villa, the house, ancillary buildings, farm and gardens that today make up Llanerchaeron are now recognised as one of the earliest works of architect John Nash. For the best part of 20 years the Trust has been painstakingly restoring and reviving the fortunes of this charming estate under the dedicated stewardship of Paul Boland, who has been there from the start.

For several years Nash's association with Llanerchaeron was speculative. There are few records from the time, but the chance discovery of a receipt for glass, hidden away in the loft, at last confirmed an enduring suspicion. Even though

exact details and plans have not yet been found, either at the house or within the wider Nash archive, we might assume that given his brief, Nash, like his good friend and associate Humphry Repton, would have had a hand in the wider specification of the estate as a whole. He might well have produced a vision encompassing the house, its parkland and the existing home farm.

Nash first came to Llanerchaeron in 1795 at the request of Major William Lewis. His brief was to remodel an earlier seventeenth-century house and provide a further range of service buildings to serve and support the family and their growing social, agricultural and, importantly, horticultural ambitions. As well as casting his eye over the finer details of their modest yet comfortable home, Nash doubtless also set about rethinking and expanding the facilities in the existing home farm, just a stone's throw from the house. This involved simultaneous alterations to several existing farm buildings to create a new stable block, a coachman's cottage and a carriage barn, as well as extending and incorporating various cattle barns and storage buildings into a harmonious whole. One of the great joys of Llanerchaeron is that, as it has remained in the same family until its donation to the Trust in the 1990s, much priceless detail has survived, albeit often in need of restoration. The result is an estate in its entirety which possesses, on a small scale, all the key elements we might expect to find in much grander country houses.

LEFT The fernery at Llanerchaeron is said to be the oldest in the country. Its restored ferns enjoy the cool shade between outside of the western wall and the towering tree screen of the pleasure grounds.

OPPOSITE Clues in both materials and style determine that the most westerly garden was the first to be built here, followed at some stage by the eastern garden, which is still in part overlooked by the earlier farm buildings beyond.

Importantly for us, Nash's attention was also focused on the provision of at least one, if not two, walled gardens. They are located a short walk from the house and screened by a small pleasure garden of towering oaks, beech and rhododendron. Covering together some 1½ acres (0.6ha), the walled gardens at Llanerchaeron form the southern boundary of the farm complex; they were ideally situated to make best use of the farm manure. The additional space behind the northern face of the great wall also allowed for frame yards, bothies and storage. The western garden, by far the most interesting and complex, must surely have been part of Nash's plan. Except for the northern wall, faced on the outside in cheaper local stone, the remaining walls are built entirely of brick, sourced from clay pits on the estate – an ambitious and sizeable investment. Its neighbouring eastern partner was clearly a slightly later build, as even a cursory glance at the junction of the brickwork will reveal, but, whether separated by days, months or a few years, there is no doubt that both gardens were extremely productive for very long periods of time.

The garden, as originally built, had in its north-western corner, within its south-facing wall, a simple series of flues. These were served by fire pits, sited originally beneath open-sided lean-tos which themselves opened out to the frame yard and pineapple pits beyond. The early visitor to the garden would have enjoyed a leisurely, if short, stroll through the pleasure gardens towards the great wall of the garden itself, drawn to a single low, wide door in its western side. Running away southward, in the shadow of this western border and the pleasure garden, was an ornate fernery, now reinstated and thought to be among one of the oldest in Britain. Why the main entrance was not set into the centre of this wall is not clear. Yet it almost certainly opened out into a garden classically divided into quadrants with an off-centre dipping pool, but with a further circular service pathway running below the walls.

Sadly there are no records to tell us what was planted where at Llanerchaeron. However, we are helped in some measure by the survival of several espaliered fruit trees, and our knowledge of conventions in many other similar gardens. The fruit trees here are still productive; they help to divide the gardens and may in some cases be around 200 years old.

At the time of their construction in the late 1790s, the gardens at Llanerchaeron would have made use of many contemporary ideas. Hotbeds and pineapple pits were incorporated into a frame yard, but without written records it is hard to know whether there was an original plan for a glasshouse. The sun-soaked south face of the north wall today carries all the scars of successive evolutions of glasshouses, inspiring the architectural detective within us to make sense of the sequence of events. The wall height here has almost certainly been raised from the original, suggesting that glass was a later addition. It is certain too that the wall was heated through additional fire pits and flues, which survive today in the remodelled bothies and workshops behind. The current wall is dominated by a post-war concrete greenhouse, but we can deduce when the Victorian heating system of hot water pipes was installed.

We know that the bailiff's house, which now sits on top of the wall, was built hurriedly in 1863 to afford the newly married bailiff a home. So worried were the family that the bailiff might leave if they could not accommodate him that money was thrown at the problem. The answer was to

In the absence of detailed historic notes and plans, the planting scheme in any restoration is always open to interpretation. These raised herb beds may not be original, but they offer interest and purpose while also occupying a large area, transforming an empty stretch of garden with life and vigour.

extend one of the earlier great barns, filling in a
gap that existed between it and the northern wall
of the garden. Significantly, the chimneys put up
for this new house were also in the style of that
built to house the new boiler. Thanks to the chance
recording of a wedding, it is thus clear that by
the early 1860s the walled gardens were still being
substantially developed and invested in. Much of
the original pipework survives, as do many other
features on this much-altered wall. Making sense of
the events it records is to understand how the gardens
developed, from a simple walled enclosure with
limited heated walls to a space able to accommodate
ever more glass for an increasing range of produce.
Peaches, vines and other exotic fruits were all at
some point produced here – an achievement all
the more remarkable because of Llanerchaeron's
relatively secluded setting, near the west Wales
coast. It is said that the family regularly entertained
Lord Milford, a prominent member of the local
gentry, and the delicacies presented must have been
a great testament to the skill of the gardeners and
the productivity of the garden, located as it is in a
climate of great seasonal extremes.

Both gardens have a dipping pool, although the
later, eastern one may have contained fish; both are
fed through underground clay pipes from the small
lake to the south-west. The lake itself begs many
questions, looking in plan as if it might have been
extended at some time. Perhaps first built with the
island in its centre, its westerly extension may have

OPPOSITE The ponds are fed via clay pipes from the nearby lake. Other methods for obtaining a water supply include digging a well, using a spring and harvesting rainwater.

RIGHT The reconstructed gardeners' latrines are a fun demonstration of how detailed restoration can evoke the day-to-day lives of past generations of gardeners.

been deliberately engineered to aid the planting in the eastern garden just above it. The lower stone wall that now encloses this garden was almost certainly not part of the original design, prompting the question as to why the garden might have been left 'open'. In the walled garden at Ickworth in Suffolk, there has been some speculation that the canal – which runs along its base and forms the southern border of the garden, in the absence of any walls – was put in to reduce the effects of frost. The relatively warmer water would, it is now thought, have helped to keep the frost at bay, acting rather like a night storage heater. It is tempting to speculate that the same idea was employed at Llanerchaeron, albeit for a limited period.

As the restoration of house and gardens continues, Llanerchaeron is coming back to life. Twenty years ago its gardens were virtually abandoned and their creator unknown. Today, as we piece together their complex story, the walled gardens of this model estate once again enclose a world in which a magical sense of order and productivity has started to revive.

LEFT One of Llanerchaeron's endearing features is its doorways. Notably both wide and low, they have easily accommodated generations of gardeners and their barrows down the centuries.

WATER AND THE WALLED GARDEN

'Water, water everywhere!' If only it was always that easy. As any gardener will tell you, watering the right amount at the right time is the key to any successful plot. These days, of course, we have pressurised water systems and cheap hose to transport it wherever needed. During the recent reconstruction of the walled garden at Blickling Hall in Norfolk, a comprehensive network of pipework was laid to standpipes right across the plot before any new planting was undertaken.

Yet in most kitchen gardens water was literally at the centre of their planning and construction. Often as not, a central pool or dipping pond was built right in the middle, allowing easy access for buckets and watering cans. At Llanerchaeron an earlier dipping pool was complemented by an additional carp pool in the neighbouring walled garden.

In this case both pools were fed via clay pipes from the nearby small lake, itself an artificial creation. Where natural watercourses were absent, wells were dug instead. In many gardens the building of glasshouses offered the chance to harvest rainwater into tanks within the glasshouse, which were sometimes given hand pumps too. The location of many glasshouses at the higher, northern side of a garden also helped: their water tanks and cisterns could deliver water around the southern end of the garden with the help of hose pipes and gravity. This ready source of water capture aided day-to-day irrigation within what were usually hot and humid houses. It also helped to maintain water levels within the closed water heating systems that by the mid-Victorian period were pumping warm water around glasshouses, thanks to coal- or wood-fired boilers set below ground level.

Water could still be moved by hand, of course, and not simply with a bucket or can. One simple invention to assist the poor soul tasked with dispensing hundreds of gallons during a hot summer's day was the water barrow. This consisted of a wheeled iron carriage in which was suspended a large galvanised drum; it was mounted on two pivots to keep level in transit, but could also be tipped to pour if large quantities of water were required. Many examples of water barrows still survive. Some are in working condition; others remain as sentinels in restored gardens, sometimes repurposed as planters, sometimes as rather forlorn relics in the corner of a forgotten border or reclamation yard.

OPPOSITE, CLOCKWISE FROM LEFT The dipping pond at Arlington Court, Devon provides a serene focal point, now notably undisturbed by gardeners with their cans or buckets; water pours constantly into this trough at Easton Walled Gardens, Lincolnshire, providing an alternative to the classic dipping pond; the restored central pond at Beningbrough Hall, North Yorkshire.

LEFT The water barrow was a simple but effective way of moving water around the garden, a task we take for granted today thanks to hosepipes and pressurised water.

130

BERRINGTON HALL

Herefordshire

As we have seen, gaining an accurate historic picture of how any walled kitchen garden has developed over its lifetime can prove difficult, even where records exist. Berrington Hall in Herefordshire is a good example of how tracing the evolution of a large, well-established garden may involve more than a search through the archive. When possible, some high-tech archaeology can also be invaluable for a thorough garden investigation.

In 1775 Thomas Harley, a local man who made a fortune in London as a banker and merchant, bought the Berrington Hall Estate. Almost immediately he commissioned none other than 'Capability' Brown to redesign the landscape, complete with all the elements befitting the family seat of a man celebrating his success. By 1778 Brown had persuaded Harley to engage his son-in-law, Henry Holland, to design a new neoclassical house that made the best of the views, and by 1784 their work was largely complete. The essential Brownian components of house, vistas, lake, ha-ha and, importantly, walled kitchen garden had all been built. Contemporary visitors spoke highly of the results, among them Viscount Torrington, who described Berrington in 1784 as 'just finished and furnished in all the modern elegance, commanding beautiful views, a fine piece of water, and ... throughout a scene of elegance and refinement'.

Berrington's surrounding parkland and its walled gardens are unique for several reasons. Firstly, they comprise perhaps the last great 'improved'

landscape that Brown designed before his death in 1783, preserving many of the ideas he developed over an astonishing career. Secondly, the walled garden as it survives today is defined by a huge arc of wall at its northern end, which is extremely rare. Thirdly, we are fortunate that not only do many important cartographic sources survive at Berrington, but they have become the subject of a detailed research project seeking to revive this very special walled garden.

The importance of Brown's legacy to Berrington is a central pillar of its ongoing development. For David Bailey, the National Trust's General Manager for Herefordshire, the chance to understand fully the history of the garden has become something of an obsession, one shared by head gardener Nick Winney and project manager Ellie Jones. When I met them their research was reaching its peak, after focusing on a fascinating mix of cartographic evidence, a uniquely detailed survey of the walls and a revealing archaeological investigation.

The first task was to understand what, if anything, remained of Brown's eighteenth-century garden. Berrington's garden today, when seen from above, appears to be square, but is topped off with an enormous semi-circular enclosure at its northern

Doors and doorways are a great excuse to create an impression. While many were simple and solid, at Berrington Hall ornate wrought ironwork is used to great effect. Not only does it allow good airflow, it keeps out the pests while providing a tantalizing glimpse of the garden within.

end, bounded by a sweeping brick wall just over 13ft (4m) in height. The walled kitchen gardens cover some 3 acres (1.2ha), at least one of which is within the perimeter of the curved northern portion. Since early last century this area has been used as a farmyard, ever since the impressive stable block to the north-west burnt down.

It was also at this time that the estate passed from the Rodney to the Cawley family, against a background of gambling debts and alleged arson. The change in ownership seems to have brought renewed stability to Berrington. Apart from the stableyard, most of what they bought is represented on the very detailed Ordnance Survey map of 1887. It is clear from this just how big a concern the walled gardens were, and how they must have been prized across successive generations, first of Harleys and then Rodneys prior to the Cawley purchase.

Nothing remains in terms of any plans that Brown may have drawn up. However, we know that his foreman, Samuel Lapidge, was sent to survey the park, and bills totalling £1,600 for his and Brown's work attest to their presence here. A plan from 1815 may yet reveal the garden that Brown designed.

When sufficiently enlarged, this early nineteenth-century map shows the park and its range of buildings and features at the time of the battle of Waterloo. We see the house, a collection of four outbuildings (where the later stableyard was built), and the walled garden encompassed by a thin mauve line that denotes the signature Brownian

Despite decades as a farmyard, the sweeping curve of Capability Brown's original garden is clear to see, as is the outline of the later Victorian garden that was superimposed below it. Beyond, the house and park remain as one of the last of Brown's great improved landscapes of the late eighteenth century.

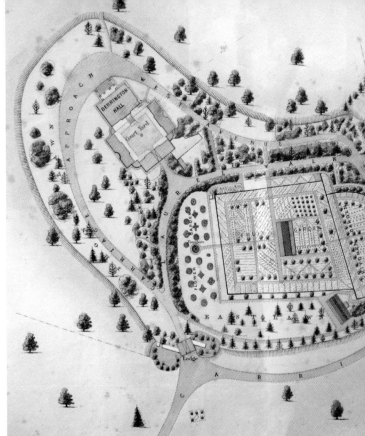

ha-ha. Closer inspection of the walled garden shows the great curved wall that runs down to a square southern portion; a potting shed or similar structure already stands along the northern side of the southern boundary. The walled garden outline, resembling a medieval helmet, steps inwards on the eastern side, allowing the construction or accommodation of a large rectangular feature that we now know to have been a conservatory. Recent research suggests that the conservatory was built at the same time as the garden wall, a deliberate feature of the pleasure ground and circular walk design. Sales particulars from 1887 suggest that it was a substantial stone and timber building, clearly placed not just to enjoy views, but to be visible from the road to the east.

My visit to Berrington was well timed. A small team from Wessex Archaeology were busy digging some trial pits. They intended to investigate several features revealed in a recent geophysical survey,

commissioned to inform future restoration plans. Using ground radar, the team clearly picked up the outlines of earlier pathways shown on the 1887 map, as well as the large foundations of the conservatory in what is now the car park. Careful excavation revealed the gentle camber of paths topped with pea-gravel, over a hardcore base of broken stone just below the surface. The survival of these paths is remarkable, given how easily they might have been dug over once buried with later layers of soil.

Armed with both the late nineteenth-century plan and that from 1815, we set about studying the brickwork and exploring the extent of the striking curved wall to the north. It was clear that the much larger square enclosure that now forms the main productive garden, separated by the central line of the potting shed, was later than Brown's original. Those responsible for building it had decided to realign the southern half and layout of the late eighteenth-century garden as designed by Brown.

OPPOSITE These simple cloches are doing a sterling job on a crisp winter's day. Behind them, the south-facing wall may once have been covered in peaches, as the remaining screen brackets that run along the wall would suggest.

ABOVE LEFT This colourful map from 1887 shows the large scale of the walled gardens at Berrington Hall.

BELOW LEFT The similarity between Berrington and the 5½ acre (2.2ha) garden at Combermere Abbey in Cheshire, built at least a century later, is striking. It's tempting to think that Brown's design might have been an influence.

A recent brick survey, which many gardens would benefit from, concurred with our findings. It also identified two distinct patterns of brick courses: a Flemish garden bond used in the earlier curved wall, and an English garden bond employed in the later structure.

An important clue as to when this dramatic change occurred is inferred from a further plan that dates to 1825 – the first time that the new arrangement was recorded. It follows therefore that it must have been built between 1815 and 1825, representing a substantial period of investment in the estate when the original garden would have been almost 40 years old.

For David and his team, the results of their investigations have helped to describe, in broad terms, the transition from a late eighteenth-century garden of, it is thought, only around 2 acres (0.8ha), to one which, thanks to a timely redesign, flourished throughout the Victorian period. They have conclusively shown that the garden's most distinguishing feature, its huge curved wall, survives as a stunning example of Brown's capability, flair and imagination, preserved within what is almost certainly one of last great landscape and architectural commissions he undertook. They now hope to remove the farmyard that has dominated this space for over a century and restore it to the highly productive garden it once was – an ambition the great man would surely welcome.

The base of the 'D' divides the garden north and south. A range of glasshouses once adorned this sun-covered southern face, which must once have included a vinery. Traces of low brick arches have recently been found in the bed below, which would have allowed the roots of the vine to make their way into the vinery from beds just out in front. Behind it the old back sheds survive, complete with tool store and boiler house.

139

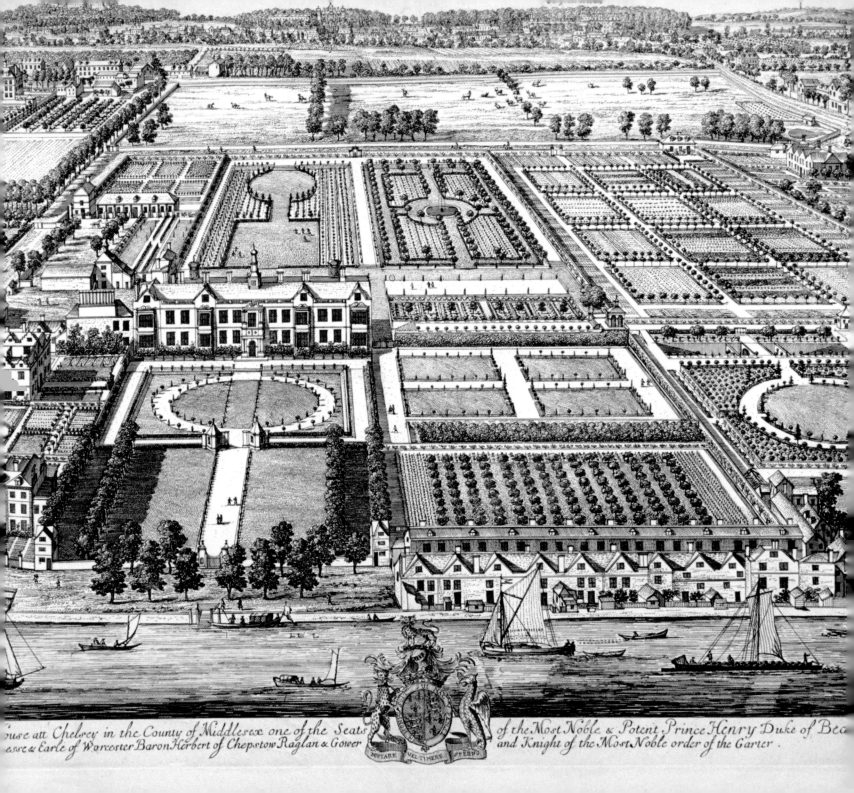

ouse att Chelsey in the County of Middlesex one of the Seats ... of the Most Noble & Potent Prince Henry Duke of Bea
esse & Earle of Worcester Baron Herbert of Chepstow Raglan & Gower ... and Knight of the Most Noble order of the Garter.

MUTARE VEL TIMERE SPERNO

In studying the walled kitchen garden, it is perhaps easy to assume that everything within it originated on the estate and in the hands of gifted head gardeners. In truth, from the late seventeenth century onwards, both walled gardeners and the great landscape designers relied upon a growing number of commercial nurseries to furnish their gardens and estates with enormous quantities of seeds, plants and trees, both native and exotic. That they could do so in such large numbers, and with such high-quality products, demonstrates an established expertise which helped drive, and was itself driven, by the horticultural renaissance of the eighteenth century.

Most of the landed gentry also owned large houses in London, historically the epicentre of high society, gossip and developing trends. Many would have owned a walled kitchen garden, and the construction of railway networks during the early nineteenth century enabled fresh produce from their country estates to be sent up to the city on an almost daily basis. It is therefore no surprise, given London's central role in society and its thriving port and markets, that the earliest plant nurseries and seed merchants began in the capital. Towards the end of the seventeenth century and during the eighteenth numerous firms were established in Brompton, Kensington, Fulham, Hackney and

elsewhere. It is perhaps hard to imagine huge swathes of today's congested urban landscape covered in walled nurseries, but their development accompanied new horticultural fashions. Ranging in size from 1 acre to 50 (0.4–20.2ha), these nurseries specialised in every kind of vegetable, plant, shrub and tree. Thousands of plants in pots were ready to be transported across the country, as were innumerable varieties of seeds. As the empire spread and more exotic tastes were imported, more ambitious firms invested in stove houses and glasshouses, employing increasing numbers of skilled nurserymen. By the mid-eighteenth century around 40 provincial nurseries had been established outside London, Caldwells in Cheshire perhaps being the most well-known.

The rise of the nursery, and the skilled nurseryman, not only helped furnish the expanding kitchen garden with plant stock; they also provided a ready supply of trained gardeners for the great estates. Some emerged as specialists in flowers, vegetables or fruit trees, others in raising plants and exotics under glass. Some estates even sent their gardeners to nurseries for apprenticeships, enabling them to bring back the latest tips and tricks. In the eighteenth century the rise of Britain's nurseries went hand in hand with the trend for 'improved' landscapes and bigger kitchen gardens.

OPPOSITE This view of Chelsea drawn in 1720 shows the London seat of the Dukes of Beaufort, surrounded by acres of gardens. It is now hard to imagine, but at the same time the neighbouring boroughs of Fulham and Kensington housed many successful plant nurseries, covering what are now some of the most affluent and built-up suburbs in Britain.

5

Gardens in the age of empire: the nineteenth century

The towering walls at Normanby Hall in Lincolnshire would easily support a traditional lean-to glasshouse, yet here they appear even higher when seen behind the unusually sited three-quarter span glasshouse range.

At the turn of the nineteenth century, Britain was the dominant global power. Despite losing the American colonies in the War of Independence, transatlantic trade remained buoyant. Financial and territorial gains in India and elsewhere offset their loss, and technological innovation fostered industrial production on an unprecedented scale.

For the walled kitchen garden, this was a time of radical change. A growing class of wealthy industrialists swelled the ranks of the upper classes, keen to buy or build their own country seats and to create their fashionable estates. The Victorians' capacity for invention and technological endeavour drove the development of the kitchen garden to new heights. From the introduction of iron glasshouses in the early part of the nineteenth century to boilers with which to heat them, bigger and bolder was the simple rule. As horticultural adventurers brought back ever more exotic fruits, vegetables and flowers, those working in glasshouses, orchid houses and orangeries rose to meet the new challenge.

By the close of the century, the British walled kitchen garden had developed into perhaps the finest of its kind in the world. Yet for all the science and technology that such gardens now displayed, success depended upon an essential component that only experience could provide: the tried and tested skills, intuition and discipline of their gardeners.

The kitchen garden at Tyntesfield in Somerset, with its later neoclassical entrance archway.

CLUMBER PARK

Nottinghamshire

There is perhaps some irony to the story of Clumber Park. The house which its magnificent walled garden was built to serve has long since gone, leaving the park, its Gothic chapel and gardens alone to hint at the once great fortune and position of its former owners, the Dukes of Newcastle.

Completed in the mid-1770s, the house was demolished in 1938 to avoid a tax bill, but thankfully the wanton destruction ended there: when you enter the walled garden, you might think you'd arrived in its heyday. The walled kitchen gardens still cover some 4 acres (1.6ha). An astonishing swathe of glass, timber and ironwork forms the backdrop to what must be one of the biggest, most productive gardens in the National Trust's care. For Chris Margrave, the head gardener, and his dedicated team, Clumber's design and unique position as the focal point of the park give the garden a particular purpose and presence.

I came here specifically to see its defining feature, the famous Long Range glasshouse. Now beautifully restored, the structure stretches some 450ft (137m) across the south-facing wall of the garden. It is divided into 13 different sections; a towering conservatory stands in the centre, with a palm house behind. Within these sub-divisions were a vinery, a pear house, a peach house and probably space for nectarines, along with a propagation house. Built in 1910 by the legendary James Gray of Chelsea,

LEFT The perfectly symmetrical Long Range glasshouse is Clumber's crowning glory, containing figs, vines, peaches and nectarines. First built in 1910, it has been recently restored, and at 450ft (137m) is the longest glasshouse in the care of the National Trust.

OPPOSITE Clumber also houses a national collection of apple trees, focused on Nottinghamshire and other regional varieties, which thrive within its extensive walled area, along with a national collection of rhubarb.

who also designed glasshouses at Cliveden and Sandringham, it has undergone several restorations, most recently in 2014. The longest glasshouse in the National Trust's care, the building displays many of the original features that made its makers famous. Cast-iron fittings still support the whole structure and many continue to make it function, opening vents and windows with an effortless precision that modern structures might envy.

It is astonishing to think that this enormous range of glass would have been complemented by several other glasshouses too. Sadly these have not survived – some must have been earlier than Gray's monumental addition, which no doubt swept away several predecessors. Also striking is the relatively late date for such a huge investment, in the years just before the First World War, which went on to change the fortunes of so many country estates. Nonetheless Gray's new build incorporated an impressive range of buildings behind it, including gardeners' rest rooms, bothies, boiler rooms and a mushroom house, details of which survive on a plan as late as 1935.

Clumber's towering walls are, of course, its earliest feature: broadly speaking, they divide the garden into two halves, north and south. Designed by the architect Stephen Wright in 1772, the walled

The extensive stores and bothies behind the Long Range glasshouse are full of fascinating examples of equipment.

The herbaceous borders at Clumber Park contain
a glorious array of flowers, including these allium heads
and herbaceous geraniums (left), Maltese cross (top) and
penstemons (above).

ABOVE The double herbaceous borders at Clumber are the spine of the garden.

OPPOSITE The conservatory and palm house are at the heart of James Gray's design, reminding us that although highly productive, Clumber was designed to be seen and shown off to visitors.

garden offers a masterclass in aspect and location. Orientated 28 degrees to the south-east, it is protected by a huge shelter belt of trees to the north and east, while making perfect use of the park's topography. The garden slopes gently from north to south, its eastern and western halves converging at a central double border which connects the conservatory to the southerly frost gate. The garden thus achieves a near-perfect drainage pattern, as described in the *Gardener's Assistant* of 1925:

An excellent form of garden is one with a regular declivity from north to south, in which direction a walk divides the area into two equal portions, each of which slopes uniformly from the side inwards to the central walk.
Vol I, p.1.

There is a great symmetry at Clumber. Today the central walk is once again one of the highlights, serving as a key axis through the garden. Looking up from the southern end, its wide double borders have been planted in the spirit of Gertrude Jekyll: whites and purples eventually give way to oranges and yellows, drawing the eye onward between the great flanking pillars of the central east–west wall and on towards the conservatory. It is easy to imagine the Dukes and their guests enjoying a gentle stroll up this graceful avenue, relishing the delights of their private garden as they were revealed season after season.

The success of the garden today is the result of enormous efforts by Chris and his team of gardeners and volunteers. The northern half has been planted and is now bursting with produce, and the rather unconventional ground plan offered by the southern half of the garden has also been put to good use. Once again arranged with great symmetry, the southern portion is subdivided with two matching, spade-shaped enclosures; comprising small walled gardens of their own, each is secure behind high brick walls and stone doorways. To the east the garden is full of soft fruit, as it probably was originally, and the rose garden is placed to the west. The rose garden is in fact next to the earliest head gardener's house, built into and onto the western wall; a sensible arrangement as he would have been responsible for the house's daily supply of cut flowers, and would have been personally involved with roses and other floral arrangements. Such was

151

the status of the head gardener role at Clumber that it was eventually rewarded with a newer and bigger house in Victorian times – at the north-western entrance to the garden behind the Long Range Glasshouse, from where the incumbent could survey his domain. Yet, despite the importance and influence accompanying this job within the wider estate, the new house was designed to remind the occupant of his subordinate position. Grand and comfortable as it was, it lacked one key feature: a front door. Head gardener you might be, but you still had to use a staff entrance to the side.

Since its creation, Clumber Park has sought to impress its visitors with an unprecedented sense of scale. Whether through the lime tree avenue, almost two miles (3km) in length, that leads the visitor into its heart or the over-the-top chapel to demonstrate the piety of successive Dukes, or the crowning glory of its towering Long Range glasshouse, Clumber remains a delight for anyone who loves a walled garden.

Today's mixture of prolific borders and extensive orchards has created a garden that is both colourful and productive, while maintaining year-round interest within its enchanting walls.

FROST GATES

For the walled gardener, frost is a powerful enemy precisely because of the walls themselves. These defining features that harness the heat of the sun and keep out the wind and pests so effectively can also trap pockets of frost within them. Effectively they take the cold air hostage in the garden, with potentially disastrous results for crops and trees.

The cold air that creates frost is most concentrated where it sinks toward the lowest point of a garden. In most well-planned walled gardens this will be at its southern end, behind the northern side of the surrounding wall. It is easy to see how on a still and dank day the frost is unlikely to disappear if left in the shade. For many centuries gardeners, especially walled gardeners, have recognised the need to release these damaging pockets of cold air, and many walled gardens, Clumber and Knightshayes included, have frost gates to let the frost escape. These are openings in the walls: they may take the form of gates or doors, or be simple grilles. In some instances, such as at Ickworth in Suffolk, the southerly wall was left out altogether. It was replaced with a canal, not only to form a barrier to pests but also, through the temperature differential between the air and water, to prevent frost from forming in the first place.

Looking somewhat forlorn, the frost gate at Knightshayes in Devon remains a tangible example, located in the lower corner of this dramatic fairy-tale garden.

TATTON PARK

Cheshire

The walled gardens at Tatton Park are relatively unusual for the late eighteenth century. Far from being hidden away out of sight within the surrounding park, they are an integral part of the house, reflecting the passion for horticulture shared by successive generations of the Egerton family.

It is this fascination for gardening and growing that drove the expansion of the gardens here. Endowed with almost limitless space within what was once a 25,000 acre (10,117ha) estate, Tatton's gardens could expand onto the fertile Cheshire plain that it commanded. As a result, while the development of many walled gardens necessitated either their demolition or dramatic remodelling, at Tatton whole gardens were simply added to existing ones. The result is a series of three distinct walled gardens that chart changing practices and ideas, encapsulating the story of the greatest kitchen gardens across the eighteenth and nineteenth centuries.

Today an impressive 6½ acres (2.6ha) of walled kitchen gardens captivate many of Tatton's 800,000 visitors a year. They are overseen by head gardener Simon Tetlow, who came to Tatton 16 years ago to manage the reconstruction. Simon's career echoes that of many former head gardeners: a horticultural journeyman, his experience and expertise have brought him to one of the country's most popular estates. Yet back in 2001 the gardens were empty of life, lacking the beds that had once been so productive; many of the glasshouses were in a parlous state, if not missing altogether.

The house that forms the basis of the current mansion was built by John Egerton in 1716. It is highly likely that the most westerly of Tatton's walled gardens dates from this time. Covering 3½ acres (1.4ha), it is divided in two by a once heated wall, now faced on its southern side by a late Victorian glasshouse containing figs and peaches; it's tempting to think that this may have replaced an even earlier example. As Simon confirms, the flues still draw if lit, and within half an hour the bricks reach the desired temperature – the warmth of your hand if you hold it under your armpit for a minute is the walled gardener's rule of thumb. This extensive garden would have been highly productive. It has a rich layer of much improved soil and compost covering a well-draining natural layer of sand. An unusual feature stands in the south-western corner: the watchman's tower overlooked not only the garden, but also the approach to the house, giving the staff notice of the family's movements.

The early eighteenth-century mansion had been much altered and remodelled by the 1790s. Samuel Egerton, inspired by his Grand Tour, eventually engaged Samuel Wyatt to give the estate a neoclassical makeover. The vision was subsequently realised by Samuel's son, William Tatton Egerton, from 1780, while Wyatt's work was complemented by that of his nephew Lewis. The park and gardens were later embellished by the hand of Humphry

Traditional wooden beehives in the orchard at Tatton Park, Cheshire.

The Egertons'
horticultural
ambitions peaked
in the 1860s when
Joseph Paxton
designed and
built the Fernery,
creating for the
family and their
guests a surreal
tropical world
packed with exotic
species.

ABOVE The bell at Tatton not only sounded for daily breaks, it also warned the gardeners of owners and their guests approaching.

BELOW This recently restored glasshouse, full of figs and tomatoes, leans against the hot wall in the early eighteenth-century garden, though it is a later addition.

RIGHT The unusual watchman's tower would have provided security for both the garden and the approach to the main house.

157

Repton, famously described as the last great landscape architect of the eighteenth century. In 1791 Repton, then at the start of his landscaping career, produced one of his earliest famous 'Red Books' for Tatton. This beautifully bound volume is packed full of exquisite plans, sketches, watercolours and innovative overlays, providing his clients with a unique 'before and after' insight into his vision for the estate. In this Repton's approach differs from that of 'Capability' Brown, for example, whose thoughts and ideas were rarely recorded in such detail.

As well as the reworking of the wider park and its gardens, this period also saw the walled garden expanded in line with Wyatt's development of the house. Whereas Brown might have recommended demolishing and relocating the earlier walled garden, it seems Wyatt combined the two elements, not only maintaining the garden but connecting it to the house by enclosing another, which in turn linked the kitchen gardens to the stable yards beyond. Within this new enclosure Wyatt designed the earliest glasshouse in this range, the pinery and vinery, which was restored in 2007. Typically divided into three separate bays, all were connected via a walkway which ran along the south face of the garden's northern wall.

These three distinct areas allowed for the potting and careful nurturing of cuttings and young plants either side of a central, warmer bay, which housed plants due to fruit that year. With the vines spread out above, tiered beds below filled with fermenting tanner's bark, along with heated flues in the walls and hotbeds outside, provided the warm temperatures that pineapples and vines needed to flourish through the harshest winter months. In later years productivity was maintained by Victorian

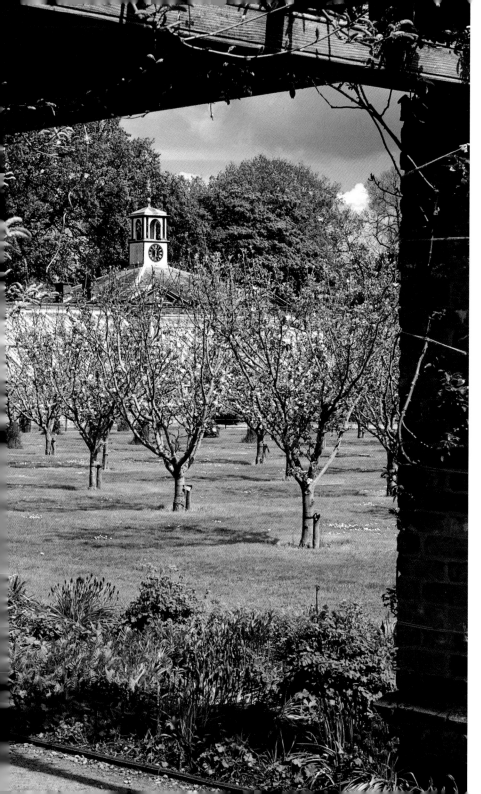

OPPOSITE ABOVE The patina on this original key to the recently restored peach cage is a poignant reminder of the gardeners who once turned it thousands of times a year.

OPPOSITE BELOW Tatton combines great architectural style with an extensive series of productive kitchen gardens that are unusually integrated within the layout of the house and formal gardens.

LEFT Orchards now occupy large areas of the gardens, making good use of space that today would be surplus to requirements. The stableyard and back sheds can be seen behind.

BELOW No kitchen garden is complete without them: terracotta rhubarb forcers offer a timeless connection between the past and the present.

boilers and hot water pipes. Recently Simon and his team have grown pineapples here again, substituting tanner's bark with barrowloads of fallen oak leaves to cosset and warm dozens of pineapple pots. By the 1830s Tatton had gained a nationwide reputation for excellent pineapples and grapes under the careful eye of a Mr Reynolds – no doubt headhunted for his expertise in glasshouse management.

The new garden also possessed a beautiful peach cage, recently restored, a frame yard, a tomato house and an orchid house – one of an eventual 20 built here just for orchids by the end of the nineteenth century. The former tomato house is now reinstated thanks to the chance find of a similar 'Herriman' glasshouse. The structure, having been rescued from Condover House in Shropshire, has been painstakingly moved and rebuilt piece by piece.

Today much of the later walled garden has been transformed into an orchard, home to 80 varieties of apple tree and some 40 types of pear. All have been sourced to reflect varieties known to have been grown in Cheshire up until 1910. The older adjacent garden is again full of kitchen garden produce, supplying the café and countless garden volunteers with seasonal delights.

Successive generations invested heavily in the garden reflecting their individual horticultural passions, in the case of William Tatton Egerton a deep love of orchids. His father, Wilbraham Egerton, had commissioned Lewis Wyatt to build the conservatory as an elegant space for relaxing and entertaining while displaying plants gathered from Australia and New Zealand. Doubtless inspired by

Tatton's kitchen garden almost certainly started here, with a hot wall behind these later glasshouses, which probably once contained dessert grapes.

Plant hunting nurtured great innovation in the design and popularity of glasshouses designed to house the rarest and most valuable specimens from around the globe, such as this one at Greenway in Devon.

PLANT HUNTERS

The growth in the development of specialist glasshouses was in large part driven by a burgeoning fascination for unusual plants. Since the turn of the century Britain's trading network and expanding empire saw a rapid increase in rare and exotic plants coming into the country. For wealthy Victorians with an interest in plant collecting, a walled garden, suitably equipped with glasshouses, was the perfect place to assemble and nurture the finest specimens, while many more were planted out in the grounds.

Popular species were camellias, rhododendrons and magnolias, although orchids perhaps inspired the greatest passion among collectors. Joseph Paxton, himself a lover of orchids, helped to enlarge the collection at Chatsworth. In the 1850s William Egerton created a stunning collection at Tatton in a purpose-built orchid house, an increasingly common feature in many Victorian gardens.

his father William, immersed in the heyday of the Industrial Revolution and certainly encouraged by his brother, a naval captain and keen plant hunter, commissioned none other than Joseph Paxton to design the Fernery in 1859.

It was thus perhaps the mid-nineteenth century that gave Tatton its crowning glory. Paxton had built the Crystal Palace for Britain's Great Exhibition of 1851, but his designs for Tatton, in the context of a private setting, were no less ambitious. Soaring iron beams support an enormous glass canopy three storeys high above rock-built beds full of ferns and towering palms; below them a network of hot water pipes maintains a tropical climate throughout the year. Simon describes the Fernery as the culmination of what decades of expert gardeners had achieved at Tatton.

For 70 or 80 years before this was built, they had perfected the art of growing some of the world's most exotic fruits with seeds and young plants from the furthest corners of the empire, developing a science that underwrites much of what we now know about horticulture. Yet this Fernery allowed them to create a corner of that exotic world, a world most who got the chance to come in here would never have had the chance to see in their lifetimes.

Tatton's survival as a garden rich in ornament, colour, architecture and production is a fitting legacy to a family whose blue blood clearly flowed through the greenest of fingers.

PEOPLE IN GLASSHOUSES

Since the orangery was established in the late seventeenth century, it was only a matter of time before more expansive glass structures were produced. The term 'greenhouse' was first used in 1664, but it was not until the mid-eighteenth century that the 'hot-house' or 'stove house' started to become an established feature of the largest walled kitchen gardens.

These early stove houses were essentially simple glass lean-tos, heated either by a hot wall or a series of underfloor flues, but preferably both. The key difference between the earlier orangery and the stove house or hot-house was that the stove was designed to be warm all year round, and heated more if necessary. In contrast, the early orangery was built simply to overwinter citrus fruits, away from the worst of the weather and frost; as such it tended to rely on the heat of the sun across its large glazed windows. With the advent of the stove, the walled gardener could at last extend the growing season through the coldest months of the year.

The striking dark green glasshouses in the 4½ acre (1.8ha) kitchen gardens on the Wimpole Estate in Cambridgeshire were reconstructed in 2000, based upon an original design by Sir John Soane.

Heating an enclosed space with the gases from open fires could, on occasion, prove problematic. Leaks into the stove house from a flue might occur, or if hot walls were absent, freestanding braziers in the heart of the orangery could also cause difficulties. Both plants and their gardeners could suffer ill-effects. Systemic difficulties in maintaining the right amount of constant heat encouraged hot-house designers to continue exploring alternative heating sources. However, it was not until the early Victorian period, and the advent of the solid fuel boiler that fed hot water through pipes within glasshouses, that the problem was finally solved.

Early lean-to glasshouses relied on the wall to support them. They required enough height to allow standing room below the eaves, as well as for vines or other plants trailed under the supports and for doorways. Where a glasshouse range has been added later, it's often possible to spot where a wall has been raised in height to accommodate the new structure – useful in assessing when and for what purpose a garden might have received further investment. As a rule, the advent of glasshouses required south-facing walls to be built to a greater height. The increase in shelter and growing space on the other walls was an added bonus, if uniform height was to be maintained.

The unmistakable sight of the dovecote at Felbrigg Hall in Norfolk, here flanked by two of the garden's glasshouses. Felbrigg remains a superb example of a large and architecturally rich kitchen garden.

165

ROBIN HOOD BOILERS

The invention of an effective heating solution
was the holy grail of glasshouse technology at the
start of the nineteenth century. A basic system
of steam heating began to replace eighteenth-
century hot walls, but by the 1840s coal-fired
boilers had been developed, capable of pumping
hot water through cast-iron pipes in a vast range
of glasshouses. Easily maintained and managed,
pipes could be laid under grilles, flags or staging,
or simply run at the base of walls. Many pipes
can still be seen in kitchen gardens today.

Several glasshouse makers also produced
boilers, the most successful of whom was
perhaps the Nottinghamshire firm of Foster
and Pearson. From 1841 onwards Robert Foster
produced glasshouses in a huge range of styles,
supported in part with cast-iron pillars which
helped to make them portable – useful if the
owner moved and wanted to take his investment
with him. Foster's business was part foundry and
part joinery, but in 1893 the company merged
with one of its major clients, the nurseryman
and horticulturalist Henry Pearson, to create
one of the most famous glasshouse brands in
the world. The firm's subsidiary, the Beeston
Foundry Company, produced a huge range of
boilers, their titles inspired by its proximity to
Sherwood Forest. The Robin Hood boiler was
initially coal-fired, but later examples in the
early twentieth century were fed by oil or gas.
It became ubiquitous as the boiler of choice, not
only in Foster and Pearson glasshouses but many
others across the country.

TYPES OF GLASSHOUSE

By the late nineteenth century, the business of glasshouse-building was well established. A range of manufacturers offered a large variety of options, many springing up following the abolition of the glass tax in 1845. Some developed from engineering companies that already specialised in boilers and ironwork. Foster and Pearson, based in Nottingham, were among the most prolific and well recognised, in part because so many good examples have survived. The company produced the ubiquitous Robin Hood series of boilers which can still be found, cold and redundant, in many gardens today.

Iron-framed glasshouses had been around since the early nineteenth century, when the properties of what was seen as a new material were first recognised. As the Industrial Revolution gathered speed, innovative production processes brought about huge changes in the quality of iron available: not only durable, it could also be cast in a broad range of shapes, achieving designs often beyond the scope of timber. In 1816

This hard-working full-span greenhouse at Tyntesfield outside Bristol is a rare galvanised example. While most through history were made of wood, from the early ninteenth century, cast-iron variations were introduced to great effect, with galvanised frames appearing toward the end of the century.

167

John Claudius Loudon, a renowned horticulturalist, designed an iron 'glazing bar' capable of taking small glazing panels. This property alone allowed for the development of graceful curved roofs, such as that on Paxton's magnificent Crystal Palace in 1851. Today iron glasshouses are rare, but those at Bicton Botanical Gardens in Devon epitomise the bold ingenuity of the period.

For all their obvious disadvantages, however, timber glasshouses remained popular. They were much cheaper to build and easier to transport, and, at a time when labour was relatively cheap, they were affordable. Some gardens had dedicated joiners and artisans to paint and repair their glasshouses, clearly a full-time job on larger estates.

By the turn of the twentieth century several firms were experimenting with materials such as galvanised steel, replacing traditional wooden frames. Glass manufacture had also improved, creating panes of greater durability and size. These greatly increased the amount of light getting into glasshouses, now less encumbered with fragile and fussy roof structures.

Through the history of the glasshouse, the figure of Joseph Paxton stands above all others. He was head gardener at Chatsworth in Derbyshire, but it was his work as a garden designer and glasshouse architect that brought him fame, alongside other great Victorian engineers such as Telford and Brunel. In striving to innovate and embrace new materials, he also tried to make the results more accessible.

ABOVE AND OPPOSITE The graceful lines of the glasshouses at Bicton Park Botanical Gardens in Devon were made possible thanks to the development of cast-iron glazing bars around 1816, which could accommodate small glazing panels.

In 1858, having become an MP and being already quite well-known, Paxton championed the idea of 'hot-houses for the million'. Targeting the growing middle class, he sought to open up the world of the glasshouse using cheaper, pre-fabricated examples made from timber. Also known as 'Paxtonian Plant-houses', these were essentially pitched roofed frames available in almost any length; they formed a simple triangular section and were fully glazed.

As the century wore on, so the number of manufacturers increased. Some took up Paxton's challenge to cater for the lower end of the market, while others remained focused on the professional and upper end, chasing high-class clients and courting their agents and gardeners. A growing range of magazines and periodicals gave advice on kitchen gardening and equipment, while improved manufacturing techniques increased the choice available to amateurs and professionals alike. Galvanised buckets, plant sprays, wire for training fruit trees, hose pipes and a host of now mass-produced hand tools slowly transformed the practical side of kitchen gardening.

LEFT This glasshouse, within the walled garden at Greenway in Devon, is a unique example with rounded ends. The technical and financial challenges such designs demanded were obviously worth meeting for Greenway's most famous resident, Agatha Christie.

OPPOSITE The crisp architectural lines of this glasshouse at West Dean in Sussex are mirrored in the planting and design of the garden's central quarters.

THE GLASS TAX, 1745–1845

In 1745 the government introduced a tax on glass which, although it covered all glass goods, had a serious impact on plate glass manufacture and development in Britain. Because glass was sold by weight, manufacturers made it thinner to offset the cost, making it more brittle, which directly affected the quality and versatility of glass in hot-houses, stoves, orangeries and glasshouses. Many early glasshouses that have survived and been restored are covered in more panes of glass; they are smaller and weaker, set between numerous thin spindles. The result is a weak roof requiring substantial annual maintenance, as those who have tried to restore them will tell you.

The effect of the tax on the research and development of glass production, and consequently in its wider architectural use, was profound. It ensured that glasshouses within walled kitchen gardens were only available to the wealthiest until the tax was repealed in the second half of the nineteenth century. However, from the 1850s a huge number of glasshouse or hot-house companies joined those already established, many of whom had started out as boiler makers. Given the importance of boilers to the story of the Victorian glasshouse, it was surely no coincidence that these firms soon realised branching out into glasshouses would benefit their own businesses.

171

KNIGHTSHAYES COURT
Devon

Knightshayes was the first reconstructed walled garden that I ever saw, almost a decade ago. Since 2002 this late Victorian fairytale enclosure has been reinvigorated with great ambition and success. It has, in several ways, set the standard for many others subsequently brought back to life within the National Trust and beyond.

Surrounded by iconic and ostentatious neo-Gothic walls, its 2½ acres (1ha) of beds and borders were once complemented by some 1¾ acres (0.7ha) of sheds, bothies and glasshouses, the last of which are now sadly long gone. However, the garden and its principal buildings have been carefully restored and do real justice to its unique surroundings.

Built towards the end of the Victorian period and the heyday of the walled kitchen garden, Knightshayes combined many of the key principles established by previous generations of walled gardeners. Architecturally it bears the unmistakable hand of the flamboyant, sometimes controversial architect William Burges, who created the extraordinary mansion just to the south, but in terms of layout its designer was Edward Kemp. He had served an apprenticeship under Joseph Paxton at Chatsworth House, and during the 1840s and 1850s became a leading authority on the design and layout of several municipal parks and gardens. In 1851 Kemp published *How to Lay Out a Small Garden*, which set out his views. Despite the title, his book actually detailed the best arrangements for walled kitchen gardens of major estates, such that by 1869 he was approached to infuse the new garden at Knightshayes with the latest ideas and features.

On the other hand, William Burges's vision for his client, John Heathcoat-Amory, the 1st Baronet, was of an estate imbued with his own passion for bizarre medieval splendour. His commission was to knock down the existing house and ancillary features within the park, including the original walled garden that it's thought stood on the site of

OPPOSITE Any visitor to Knightshayes will be struck by the heady mix of industry and order that this highly productive garden offers at any time of year.

PAGES 174–175 The garden's unique aspect within a steep fold of the park is highlighted from every angle by the staggered lines of its surrounding walls, the tops of which are coped in thousands of specially made clay tiles.

the present mansion, and redesign from scratch. Work began in 1869, and by 1874 the house and main elements were largely complete, with the notable exception of the proposed medieval interiors. These in particular were finally to cause the family and Burges to part company with some acrimony, Burges's designs being at odds with his client's more muted tastes. However, Kemp oversaw the design of the formal gardens as well as the kitchen garden, and we might thus assume that Burges must have consulted him on its location within the estate. This certainly accords with Kemp's advice.

… a kitchen garden should be placed in the rear of the house and be as near as possible to both it and the stables … The reason of these things is plain and simple. As a kitchen is itself generally kept at the back of the house and a kitchen garden has to be in communication with it, the two should be in close proximity. The manure also from the stables having to be used in the kitchen garden ought to be capable of being readily applied and hence the desirableness of connecting the two parts as nearly as can be done.
How to Lay Out a Small Garden, E. Kemp, 1851, p.323–4

LEFT Compared to the rest of the garden's design, the main gate from the park is refreshingly understated. Perhaps its off-centre position next to the fairy-tale south-western turret was designed not to distract from Burges's signature medieval style.
OPPOSITE Knightshayes gardeners both past and present have sought to innovate, each generation making the garden their own. Here a young vineyard is becoming established, a nod towards the role of the glass vinery, now long gone.

ABOVE A bed of astilbe and echinops gives colour to the walled garden at Knightshayes.

OPPOSITE ABOVE Cut flowers dry above one of the bothies. Dried flowers were another means of extending the cut flower season right through the winter.

OPPOSITE BELOW None of the original glasshouses survive, yet important clues remain, such as these huge glazed cold frames in a corner of the frame yard.

If Kemp was responsible for placing the garden within the park adjacent to the stables, with their stunning three-dimensional aspect, it was Burges who created it in the style of the house. At its southern end he adorned the corners and main entrance for those approaching from the park and stables with two fanciful turrets. These skilfully join the walls together, seamlessly accommodating a potentially awkward architectural junction where the diving topography rises northward to a series of great terraces. The walls are built from local stone but topped with purpose-cast coping bricks that project generously over the wall, just as Kemp recommends. He was also clear about the need to create a working area out of site of the main garden, where stores and frame yards could be hidden away.

Somewhere at the back of the kitchen garden one or more sheds will be wanted for a variety of uses together with a yard for rubbish, manure, compost etc. and which last should be accessible at some point with a horse and cart.

At Knightshayes, Kemp and Burges between them set about creating the ultimate garden, which made the best of the park and its location. Key to the success of their design was the clever use of three terraces, created to overlook the garden and the park beyond towards the house. Topped with crenellated yew that once divided the garden into its quadrants, the first of these terraces was filled with ornamental planting; access to it was graced by two fabulous topiary talbots flanking the steps on the western pathway. On the second terrace, behind the northern boundary of the main garden, was the service yard. It had wide gates to the west and offered access to bothies, stores, offices and boiler rooms still in use today, as well as a way to the upper terrace via a huge ramp at the eastern end. Here were glasshouses, described with enthusiasm by the *Gardeners' Chronicle* after a visit in 1882.

We notice an extensive range of new garden offices … consisting of young men's rooms, fruit rooms, packing and potting sheds and other offices. What is called the middle range of glasshouses stands opposite these, and consists of an early and late vinery, and tomato house where the chief variety known is the 'New Dedham Favourite'.

The glasshouses as described were unusually sited, behind the outbuildings and offices. However, other glasshouses and a palm house were built on the south side of this range, overlooking the eastern half of the garden, but were relatively short-lived. Once this series of glasshouses had been demolished, the lower terrace was given over to beds and planting similar to the main garden.

However, Knightshayes's crowning glory was its upper range of glasshouses. Laid out in the form of an E rotated through 90 degrees and facing south, this stunning range was located to the east of the frame yard on the upper terrace. It would have created a magnificent backdrop to the garden, glinting in the sunshine and doubtless visible for some distance to anyone approaching from the park. Today only the foundations survive, but in time even these may be rebuilt. As originally planned, there was clearly no shortage of glass at Knightshayes; much of that on the upper terrace survived until the 1980s. Yet such a large amount of glass brings with it the need for extensive maintenance, and this must have determined the eventual decline of the glasshouses here, well within a century of them having been built.

Today the garden is in the hands of Bev Todd, Sam Brown and Lucy Halliday. Sam, who showed me around when I visited, explained that they rely on an army of some 40 volunteers to keep the garden thriving. Making the best of the nuances of its unique aspect, they are planning to plant plums and sour cherries in the cooler, north-facing shade of the lower wall, alongside an established and bountiful rhubarb patch. The flourishing central section is full of everything from cut flowers and pumpkins to classic salad crops; even a new, modest vineyard is rapidly establishing itself.

The story of Knightshayes combines great architectural and horticultural ambition. The result was a garden that reflected many of the lessons from the past as it boldly stamped its personality on the future. The two men who designed and built it created something quite unique, now recognised as one of Britain's most iconic walled gardens. For William Burges, its ebullient and uncompromising architect, this is a legacy of which he would be proud. Edward Kemp would revel in the survival of Knightshayes as a near-perfect working example of all that he'd sought to pass on – the best of both past and present for a Victorian kitchen gardener.

MUSHROOM HOUSES

Walled kitchen gardeners of the past clearly went to some trouble in designing and building spaces dedicated to the successful harvesting of fresh mushrooms. Many made special provision for their sowing and cropping all year round. The mushroom house was thus an important addition to many kitchen gardens, helped by the relative ease with which space and dark, damp conditions could be provided. Often the shaded northern area behind the south-facing wall, among the bothies and other stores, was ideal.

I have not yet seen a working mushroom house on my travels, but, where these structures do survive, their sturdy and elaborate shelving has often been brought back to use, providing valuable storage. Mushroom houses of the early nineteenth century were fitted with wooden shelves, but the combination of fresh horse manure and the compost needed to grow mushrooms caused many to rot. At Knightshayes a good example from the late nineteenth century has been retained. Cast iron supports, produced by the old firm of Tessimond and Kissack in Liverpool, carry heavy slate beds that would once have been filled with a much compacted and seeded combination of compost and dung; if kept sufficiently moist, this would produce a supply of mushrooms throughout the year with very little effort. Early mushroom houses were sometimes created in existing forcing houses, already dark and damp, while many later mushroom houses were also used to force rhubarb and sea kale, both relishing the humid, dark conditions.

The well-preserved mushroom house at Knightshayes was a model of late Victorian design, combining cast-iron framework and sturdy slate panels, a far cry from earlier timber examples.

181

6

Decline and fall: walled gardens in the twentieth century

This border, at Hinton Ampner in Hampshire, is so well-tended and established today that it's hard to imagine such a place abandoned and left to fend for itself.

Only a century ago most of Britain's walled kitchen gardens, both large and small, seemed to have a secure future. The First World War forced the country to exploit its resources and maximise agricultural output. Self-sufficiency would keep Britain from starvation.

However, the war effort also accelerated the mechanisation of Britain's landscape. The war had been the catalyst for a farming revolution, transforming the future of food production. Fresh food could now be shipped around the world, and by the 1920s economic arguments for maintaining many of Britain's largest walled gardens were beginning to wane. Rising wage bills, plus a shortage of apprentices and skilled hands, forced the gradual contraction of the kitchen garden, leaving only the biggest and wealthiest estates to carry on, maintaining many of the skills and practices we value today.

Within a generation, what had seemed an assured future looked increasingly uncertain. Yet some gardens still saw considerable investment. Attingham Park's glasshouses were replaced in 1924 and, while they remain undated, those at Plas Newydd may well have been put up at the same time. Winston Churchill, celebrated as both a leader and a gardener, built his own walled kitchen garden in the late 1920s, even as many others, such as Heligan, entered their twilight years.

Social and economic pressures on the largest gardens were compounded by the great depression and the Second World War, and by the late 1940s many estates faced crippling death duties. Large numbers were sold or even deliberately demolished; others were given over to charitable care, for instance Blickling Hall, an early donor property of the National Trust. By the 1960s most gardens had ceased to provide produce for the original house. Instead they were given over to market garden enterprises, Christmas tree farms and orchards, or were simply grassed over. With remarkable speed, a tradition of gardening hundreds of years in the making had virtually ceased to exist.

At Chartwell in Kent, a view common to almost all vibrant kitchen gardens: bamboo canes stand ready to support peas and beans among a bed full of crops, while fruit trees cling to the walls.

PLAS NEWYDD

Anglesey

In a chapter on gardens of the twentieth century, it might seem strange to include one created at least a century earlier. Today the gardens at Plas Newydd, the ancestral home of the Marquess of Anglesey, are now largely derelict, symbolising the fate that befell so many great gardens.

Since 1976 the house at Plas Newydd has been entrusted to the care of the National Trust. This beautiful late Georgian masterpiece attracts around 150,000 visitors a year, but few will have noticed the absence of a walled garden. The walled kitchen gardens were actually built some distance from the house to the west; they lie within the wider estate, outside the area managed by the Trust. Finding them thus required the help of the man now responsible for their care: the current Lord Anglesey and Earl of Uxbridge, Ben Paget.

The two of us met to explore gardens that appeared to cover a huge area and were full of intriguing features. I'd managed a glimpse of the gardens a few years previously, and remembered them as largely overgrown, with buildings in a poor state of repair. With limited knowledge of the garden, Ben was also keen to find out more. Together we set about exploring a genuinely lost garden, a foray that would lead us deep into the family archive and Ben's ancestral past.

Today the kitchen gardens cover 3½ acres (1.4ha) – made up, to my surprise, of not one, but two distinct areas, one earlier than the other. We

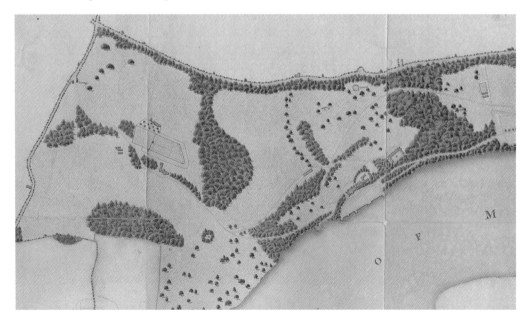

LEFT This 1804 map shows the gardens we see today. The decision to add to the existing western garden with a larger enclosure put the kitchen gardens in a far better location.
RIGHT The eastern wall of the earlier garden, with its Gothic tower and the overgrown later garden beyond.

began our search in the earlier garden, empty apart from a pony calmly grazing its 1½ acres (0.6ha). According to a former farmhand the land had been used more recently as an orchard; nail holes in the walls testified to the presence of dozens of espaliered fruit trees, now lost. The interior face of the walls was lined with brick, the exterior built of stone. In the south-east corner a stone-built apple store lay empty. In the eastern wall a central doorway with a two-storey tower connected the garden with its companion next door.

The tower would once have given the earlier enclosure a distinct entrance, but now looks out over a tangled, overgrown jungle. A quick glance at the junction of the gardens' walls confirmed that this later garden was built entirely from brick. What's more, it was obvious from the shattered remains of the glasshouse range alongside the south-east-facing wall that this garden had, until relatively recently, been well cared for. As we made our way around the remains of an old garden centre that had occupied a corner of this once enormous space, its size became apparent. Covering 2 acres (0.8ha), a great double gateway had provided service access to the east, while the eastern corner had been given a graceful curve, softening its appearance when approached from the house. In the garden's heyday the woodland now surrounding it would not have existed, but today the trees are choking the garden, both inside and out.

The glasshouses are fascinating. What appeared to be a relatively modest pinery, vinery and peach

house had clearly been added to the south-facing wall. The floor level had been raised to accommodate the underfloor pipe runs, fed from a later boiler house built among the back sheds on the northern side; it still contained its boiler under a collapsed roof. Such an addition would often have prompted work to increase the height of the wall on which the rafters of a traditional lean-to glasshouse were seated, but here a different solution was used. The walls would remain as they were, and instead three-quarter span glasshouses were built. The chance find of a nameplate told us that they were

OPPOSITE In the absence of any other records, the chance find of this nameplate in one of the ailing glasshouses revealed the makers to be the well-known Edinburgh firm Mackenzie and Moncur, probably from the early twentieth century.

LEFT The tower gateway that once formed the main entrance to the earlier eighteenth-century walled garden. Since 1804 it has been the threshold between this earlier and now empty garden, and the later, much larger brick-built enclosure that contains the glasshouse range and back sheds.

designed and installed by Mackenzie and Moncur, the great Edinburgh-based hot-house makers. Given that their business did not start until 1869, we slowly began to piece together the evolution of Plas Newydd's lost kitchen gardens. In the end, it came down to three vital maps.

In 1782 Ben's ancestor, the 1st Earl of Uxbridge, inherited Plas Newydd – then a secondary home, the primary seat being at Beaudesert in Shropshire. Nonetheless, his tenure saw a substantial investment in the estate, helped in large part by the Earl's share in Anglesey's copper mines, by the 1790s supplying a third of Britain's copper. An early estate map, dated to 1798, shows the first walled garden we explored with a neat quadrant of beds. It may have been built much earlier, possibly during the seventeenth century, solely for the neighbouring farmhouse of Llanedwen, which survives just to the south-west.

At some point prior to the creation of this map, Llanedwen was acquired by the Plas Newydd estate. It seems likely that the main house overlooking the Menai Strait was supplied by an earlier garden, now demolished, its exact location unknown. However, we do know that the 1st Earl's agent, a Colonel Peacocke, was kept busy proposing and overseeing numerous improvements to the house and its surroundings between 1792 and 1817. Working alongside the architect James Wyatt, among others, these included building a new stable range in the Gothic style, designed to be visible from the Straits, and making many additions to the mansion.

He also invited Humphry Repton to Plas Newydd in 1798. Like Wyatt, Repton had worked for the Earl at Beaudesert, and it seems he was asked to embellish further the landward approach to the house through the parkland. Contained in one of his famous 'Red Books', although sadly without its drawings, are Repton's recommendations to create a new kitchen garden to the north. He proposed to abandon the existing one, presumably because the new stableyard to be built in the general vicinity of the proposed new location would provide an ample source of manure.

Interestingly, however, although some of Repton's ideas were implemented by Peacocke, among them landscaping the main drive, many were not – including his suggestion to move rather than develop the existing walled garden. Instead, Peacocke demolished an extant farmyard to the west of the house, clearing up the view of the landscaped park. Ignoring Repton's proposal, he not only added a new, entirely brick-built enclosure to the existing garden, as shown in a plan of 1804, but also by 1815 had expanded the home farm complex adjacent to its northern boundary. With great flair, Peacocke's plan kept the garden out of sight of the new landscaped grounds, yet made use of the earlier kitchen garden. In expanding this garden, he exploited the ideal location for a new home farm to support the kitchen garden well into the future.

The 2nd Earl, who succeeded in 1812, was made the 1st Marquess of Anglesey in 1815 following his bravery at the battle of Waterloo. By this time the

walled kitchen gardens were well established at the heart of the estate. The garden was well maintained and saw considerable investment towards the turn of the twentieth century, as the later glasshouses demonstrate. An aerial photo from 1965 shows the garden still very much in production, but since the 1970s its decline has been rapid.

Today the garden is as we found it, but hopefully not for long. Nearly 240 years since the 1st Earl of Uxbridge took over Plas Newydd, his successor Ben Paget is hopeful that this beautiful walled garden and the home farm that once supported it, might once again become productive and valued features of the estate. Not only are the walls in relatively good condition, but the main elements of the glasshouses could be repaired and restored. What's more, lying sleepily beneath the undergrowth that threatens to engulf it all, is a rich and fertile soil that's been over 200 years in the making. What better start could an old garden have?

THE LOST GARDENS OF HELIGAN
Cornwall

Of all Britain's walled kitchen gardens, the once lost gardens of Heligan surely require the least introduction. Tragically abandoned at the end of the First World War, its owner haunted by the deaths of so many men from the estate and gardens, Heligan's fate epitomised that of many other gardens in the twentieth century. Yet for the last 25 years these gardens, revelling in a remarkable transformation, have welcomed thousands of people from around the world.

Rediscovered and then reconstructed to celebrate their historic and horticultural value, Heligan has become a beacon for the renovation of many other walled kitchen gardens, inspired by its story.

Much has been written about the undaunted effort and vision that Tim Smit, John Nelson and their dedicated comrades brought to the project. These days, with our increased interest in walled gardens, their rescue and restoration seems like an obvious call to arms, but in 1990 there were

Heligan's northerly vegetable garden (left) is busier than ever since the original southerly walled garden (right) was reconstructed, in large part as a flower garden. The sweeping curve of the early eighteenth-century melon yard that separates these two areas can be seen here.

few precedents for such a mammoth undertaking. Perhaps the biggest challenge faced by the team lay in recognising what they had found and how important this discovery might be.

Originally planned and built around 1800 for the Tremayne family, the gardens were eventually expanded to cover 37 acres (1.5ha), set within the wider 1,000-acre (405ha) estate. Successive generations of Tremaynes indulged their horticultural interests through the nineteenth century. They invested large sums, ensuring that the restored Heligan represents one of the most complete examples of its kind in Britain.

The southern walled kitchen garden, which dates to the early nineteenth century, has largely been restored as a flower garden; complete with a once-heated vinery and peach house, its beds are beautifully divided by a network of low box hedging. Above it a unique D-shaped melon yard to the north now boasts a pineapple pit and extensive range of cold frames, tool shed and fruit store, complete with gardeners' latrines or 'thunderboxes'. By 1835 the garden had been extended northward to its present limits with the provision of a 2 acre

LEFT Pumpkins enjoying some early autumn sunshine clearly revel in the climate that Heligan's builders and gardeners managed to harness.
OPPOSITE These cold frames, which fill the melon yard, show how their bespoke 'beaver-tail' glass panes were designed to shed water to a point, keeping it away from the narrow glazing bars to prevent rotting.

(0.8ha) vegetable or 'productive' garden. Back in 1990, after nearly 70 years of neglect, none of this was visible to the pioneers. They were confronted by an impenetrable jungle of rhododendrons, tree ferns, rampant shrubs, brambles, ivy-clad walls and crumbling buildings of unknown purpose.

Yet in 1992, within two years of the start of the project, Heligan's Lost Gardens opened to the public for the first time, while the business of clearing the wider estate and pleasure grounds continued. A new generation of gardeners began the task of serious cultivation and production for which the gardens had been designed, a process requiring the rediscovery of many old skills.

Amongst the many features that recommend Heligan to me, the reinvigorated melon yard is the jewel in its crown. It is virtually impossible to reconcile the images of the overgrown and decrepit melon house that was first discovered with today's orderly and productive space, now shared with cold frames, stores and a hotbed. When I first came to Heligan this tiny yard was the magnet that drew me though the garden and pulled me back again. Here Heligan's new gardeners have achieved one of their greatest feats: the production of pineapples.

Historically the pineapple was the favourite exotic fruit of the owners of the greatest estates. The design of a smaller pineapple pit at Heligan, dating

ABOVE Gourds and squashes boast of a productive season as they mature on this shelf in the melon house.

RIGHT The melon yard is the oldest part of the garden complex, possibly dating to 1700 and containing cold frames, sheds, a melon house, and its crowning glory, a pineapple pit.

from the seventeenth century, pre-dates many larger glass lean-to pineries found elsewhere. Its excavation and subsequent restoration has afforded a rare opportunity to understand how the pineapple pit worked, essentially through head-scratching, research and eventual trial and error. Today the pineapple pit at Heligan is capable of sustaining these fickle plants in a cosy 70–75°F (21–24°C) with little more than some steaming manure, glass and welcoming Cornish sunshine. It is the only working example in Britain.

The decision even to attempt to use the pineapple pits in anything like a traditional way was a bold one. No one in recent memory had tried to harness the warming properties of manure. Answers to basic questions such as when the manure should be used, how much was needed, what type gave the best results and how long might it last as a heat source were all unknown. I've long been a fan of experimental archaeology, but am aware that in recreating the past you also risk recreating a lot of hard work. This cannot have been lost on Tim Smit, himself an archaeologist, and was certainly no surprise to Heligan's current head gardener, Iain Davies. He and his colleague Nicola Bradley gave me a fascinating guided tour of the melon yard and talked me through the use of its beautifully restored pineapple pit.

PINEAPPLES

Nurturing a pineapple plant to maturity is as much an art as a science. Their natural habitat is in Central and South America and the Caribbean, with a climate that is both hot and, importantly, humid. The challenge for the exotic grower of the past was to recreate these conditions as effectively as possible. The hotbed, used to grow tender plants throughout the winter on a bed of manure, was established practice by the end of the seventeenth century, but the pineapple pit took the idea several stages further. Essentially it combined the heat generated by rotting manure with the captive properties of a glass cold frame. Heating the glazed bed both maintained a suitable temperature and created a degree of humidity. These smaller pits worked well in a time before more direct heating systems, which could heat walls or pipes and could be effective in the larger lean-to pineries that followed them.

Excavating Heligan's pineapple pit revealed a complex construction, reliant on the free flow of warm air around its walls and below the growing bed. The bed was supported by a hypocaust network of brick pillars and slates that the Romans might have recognised. Two brick-lined manure trenches on either side of the bed were found to need 90 tons of muck, specifically horse manure. As this slowly rots down, the heat is transmitted through honeycomb walls into the glazed bed. Because pineapples take so long to fruit, the plants are kept in pots for ease of movement and to help insulate their roots. The pots are placed in deep swathes of oak tanner's bark for the winter, a technique pioneered in Holland during the seventeenth century; today oak leaves may be used to reasonably good effect. Within the pineapple pit the beds were divided between those containing cuttings, young plants and pineapples about to fruit.

These days, we all take the pineapple for granted. Readily available, it is no longer a prized delicacy. Without gardens such as Heligan, however, it would be impossible to imagine the time, trouble and money invested in growing them in the walled kitchen gardens of the privileged few. For this elite, producing pineapples was a potent symbol not just of wealth and good taste, but also of horticultural skill and ambition. Heligan, emerging from decades of obscurity and neglect, championed the skills of walled kitchen gardeners of the past. It is fitting that it remains a centre of horticultural excellence, and has become a benchmark for the reconstruction of walled kitchen gardens.

Pineapples, once the most sought-after and valuable of exotic fruits, thrive in the 24-degree heat of the rebuilt pineapple pit.

CHARTWELL

Kent

'A day away from Chartwell is a day wasted.'
Winston Churchill

In 1922 Winston Churchill, then 48 and a seasoned political figure, bought a modest 80-acre (32.4ha) estate in Kent. Chartwell would remain his home for the next 43 years until his death in 1965 at the age of 91. During that time he extended and remodelled both house and grounds, immersing himself in a creative project that sustained him through the most challenging periods of his life.

Chartwell, when the Churchills first bought it, was a traditional estate in miniature. The house, with its splendid view over the Kentish Weald, was, architecturally at least, relatively unremarkable. Yet its landscape, water features and proximity to London provided the bones of a long-term endeavour that would in time produce a small country house with all the features of the grandest. For a man born in the impressive surroundings of Blenheim Palace, these would have been very familiar.

The walled garden at Chartwell is typical of many added to estates. It was not started until 1925, and is significant not for its size or complexity, but because it was built at a time when many kitchen gardens were struggling to survive. In addition, it was not only designed by Churchill, but built with his own hands. To my knowledge, no other walled kitchen garden was so authored by its original owner. This alone would make it unique among walled gardens, but Churchill imbued it

OPPOSITE Chartwell's garden has never been completely out of production since it was built in the late 1920s.

ABOVE Churchill's prowess as a politician was not matched by his ability as a bricklayer. These brick buttresses are earning their keep, maintaining the form and purpose of the walls he painstakingly built.

with a distinction few others have ever possessed. His kitchen garden was designed to be productive, but also to be a family space in which they could entertain, hidden from the world beyond its walls.

Covering a very manageable half-acre (0.2ha), the site today aims to represent a garden that the Churchills would recognise. A year after his death both house and grounds opened to the public. The kitchen garden was largely grassed over for expediency, and supplemented in part by fruit trees, while the central grass pathway was paved, owing to the anticipated number of visitors. However, since 2004 the garden has been brought back into production. It now provides a good annual crop of fruit, vegetables and cut flowers for Chartwell's café and house.

Churchill's walled kitchen garden reveals much about him as an accessible and pragmatic builder, for whom funds were often more limited than we might expect. The quality of the brickwork to which he famously contributed is certainly less than perfect; today long stretches of the garden's walls are propped up because of a lack of decent foundations.

When seen from the outside, the bricks used look like seconds – yet we know they were selected because they matched the existing brick walls around the house. A laborious double-pitched tile coping covers the top of the wall, in between buttresses which are not always tied into the rest of the structure. All these observations to me describe a man who simply loved having a go, regardless of expertise. His fascination with detail and process, revealed through his life and office as a war leader, are perfectly in tune with his practical intuition. Churchill never sought to excuse his failings, and while his handiwork reveals much about his limitations as builder, it also portrays an undaunted gardener, designer and family man. For someone of his character, the process of creating a home through blood, sweat and tears was the motivation for buying it in the first place.

The south-west corner contains an example of how the kitchen garden reflected the family who owned it, both at home and at play. The Marycot, or Mary's cottage, built by Churchill for his fourth daughter in 1928, is a unique addition to the otherwise productive area. Complete with a mini

OPPOSITE A splash of terracotta reveals this forcer, swamped with rhubarb.

FAR LEFT The main entrance to the kitchen garden remains as Churchill designed it.

LEFT Churchill's 'have a go' approach to life is undoubtedly what made him such a formidable character.

205

Aga, it was the focus of many a family gathering; Mary is even said to have entertained Charlie Chaplin here in 1931. Of the many additions made during Churchill's time at Chartwell, most are imbued with a sense of family life and fun. The Marycot, Churchill's studio, the swimming pool, butterfly house, croquet lawn and fish ponds combine to create a garden for the enjoyment of family and friends.

This theme was continued within the walled garden when, for the Churchills' Golden Wedding anniversary in 1958, their children gave them a Golden Rose Walk comprising 28 varieties of rose. The original no longer survives, but the current planting scheme echoes the gift; it divides the garden into its two halves, while simultaneously joining it at top and bottom. Chartwell's walled garden is a simple creation that both champions imperfection and celebrates the ambition of its builder.

At a time when most walled gardens were waning, Churchill set about creating a walled kitchen garden with characteristic energy, vision

PAGES 204–205
The joy of Chartwell is that it was built to be enjoyed by what was, despite their position, a relatively modest family, a role that it served alongside its productive purpose.

and determination. Chartwell's garden is in many ways a great compromise. Its materials, scale and the quality of its construction were all a product of means, skill and necessity. Yet to me its faults are as endearing as its achievements, precisely because its author was proud to share them with whoever came to stay. Its design ensured that the garden was as focused on family fun as in providing fruit and vegetables. Churchill created a place which in its building and daily use provided space to relax and reflect, evading the public gaze in a private world that he had made his own. It remains a unique and enchanting garden whose walls reflect the irrepressible individual who made them.

OPPOSITE 'I bought a view and a house came with it,' Winston Churchill said of Chartwell.

ABOVE Sweetcorn growing in the garden at Chartwell.

7 Walled gardens of the future: the twenty-first century and beyond

A glimpse of the vast 8 acre (3.2ha) garden at Gordon Castle in Moray. When renovations are complete it may well claim to be the biggest of its kind in Britain.

The story of Britain's classic walled gardens spans at least four centuries. In their own way, each century has created a horticultural climate that influenced the gardens' development. From a burgeoning interest in growing rare and exotic plants in the seventeenth century to the eighteenth-century expansion of the walled garden and the heyday of kitchen gardening at the turn of the twentieth, these spaces have been shaped by economics, social mobility, architectural ambition and the whims of the rich and powerful. Many thousands of gardens, both large and small, were abandoned and left to the elements, but today a growing number are being returned to use. Some, in the interests of conservation, are attempting to emulate the practices of the past and recreate historic walled kitchen gardens, while others have embraced less conventional futures.

With any such project, factors of sustainability and economic sense offset any romantic vision of what these gardens once were and might again become. Large-scale renovations are always something of a financial gamble, but the fact that a kitchen garden can produce goods that have

value helps to mitigate the risks and spark innovative ideas.

Of the many gardens that I've visited in researching this book, selecting those that, for me, seem to point towards the future has been the most difficult task. Most renovated gardens have been based on a large degree of forward thinking, so what defines a 'garden of the twenty-first century'?

To my mind, the three featured in this chapter combine to represent the very best of the past, present and future. Newport House, without a doubt the most lavish private kitchen garden I have ever seen, remains true to its eighteenth-century origins. Gravetye Manor, home of a Michelin-starred restaurant, is working as hard for its future as ever it did, driven by a horticultural and culinary ambition that its inventive creator would have championed. And Gordon Castle in Moray, in seeking to return to being one of Britain's biggest and most productive walled kitchen gardens, is combining the philosophy of past gardening practice with a real sense of artistic flair and fun – factors that reflect the family and the future they hope it will secure.

There is little in this picture of a rejuvenated and productive quarter to reveal the unique elliptical enclosure that surrounds the kitchen garden at Gravetye Manor in West Sussex.

211

NEWPORT HOUSE
Herefordshire

With very few exceptions, one thing absent from Britain's walled gardens is the people who originally created them. Most gardens that have been restored are in the care of charitable trusts, or occasionally the current generation of an ancient family seat; we have little knowledge of the aims and ambitions of those who planned, owned and worked them. However, today's owners can offer real inspiration through their sympathetic insights into the past. Newport House, for instance, has not simply been recommissioned, but infused with the very best practices and materials from the past.

Newport House, built around 1712, was purchased around a decade ago by David Watt. Next to the building, then in need of serious attention, was the former walled garden, then owned by the local council, along with a couple of hundred acres of woodland and paddocks. Initially only the pony paddocks were of interest to David and his family, but acquiring them involved taking on the walled garden as well. So began a dedicated restoration project that has taken seven years and considerable vision, determination and investment.

The warm, south-facing brick facade of Newport House provides an elegant focal point in a beautiful

rolling landscape to the north of the River Wye. The gardens that surround it have been remodelled several times, but its walled garden was derelict. Overgrown and forgotten, large sections of the walls had collapsed and there was little sign of any original layout. Archive paintings and maps revealed that the current walled enclosure replaced an earlier version nearer to the house. In 1776 it was moved to its present location and was used productively until the end of the Second World War.

Like many country houses, Newport has gone through various incarnations. During the First World War it was a convalescent home for officers, and in 1919 was purchased by the Council under the Agricultural Holdings Act. The house became a sanatorium for tuberculosis between 1921 and 1951, the farmland divided into 50-acre (20.2ha) plots and leased to returning soldiers for three generations. The walled garden continued to operate until 1951, providing food to the hospital, to which the tenant farmers also supplied meat and milk. In 1951 the house was rented to the Latvian Association of Great Britain, and it is thought an old gentleman rented the walled garden to keep his chickens in! Piecemeal management of the estate continued

Abandoned and left derelict for decades, the fortunes of the walled garden at Newport House were only reversed thanks to the passion of its new owner, who has spared no expense in rejuvenating a garden that his family can rely upon.

LEFT Many of the glasshouses were built using original cast-iron components salvaged from other examples, most of which were originally built by Foster and Pearson.

ABOVE Attention to detail at Newport House extends to this handmade steel edging around the beds, topped with a solid bar. Not only is it beautiful, it's impervious to damage caused by tools and barrows and will forever neatly define the garden's layout.

OPPOSITE When seen from afar, the garden's 2½ acres (1ha) appear to dwarf the renovated gardener's bothy.

until David decided to bring all the elements back together in a stunning restoration of the house, its grounds and the wider 500 acre (202ha) estate. Yet perhaps the most striking aspect of the restoration is the fact that it has been brought back to life for its original purpose – to serve the needs of its owner, his family and his staff.

The walled garden, covering almost 2½ acres (1ha), is again surrounded by high brick walls, complemented by a productive array of glasshouses, fruit cages and industrious areas of planting. David's research, helped by some of Newport's former walled gardeners both past and present, has returned the garden to a classic quadrant layout. Planting schemes work through an annual cycle of rotation with at least one-quarter left fallow each year.

On entering the garden through its north-western door, I was struck by the amount under cultivation, given that this is a very private garden.

Notwithstanding areas that are resting, it bursts with life everywhere. The south-facing wall is covered in young peaches, protected from the frost by a brand new set of peach screens, supported by specially commissioned cast-iron brackets. These brackets were referenced from originals found at Berrington Hall, also in Herefordshire. Netting tied beneath these panels protects the plants from frost and unseasonal extremes. Rarely have such techniques, which originated in the eighteenth century, been as painstakingly revived and reconstructed as here.

This attention to detail is one of Newport's most magical features, and is found everywhere in the garden. The edging, for example, was long gone: David's team replaced it with terracotta rope edge, but soon found this vulnerable to breakage if struck by wheelbarrows. Their solution was to commission a local blacksmith to make several hundred feet of

steel edge, topped with a solid round bar, along with a plethora of boot scrapers. The gardener's bothy has received the same lavish treatment, stripped to the bone and rebuilt with the addition of a striking thatched roof. Newport's back sheds, if they had existed, were also long gone, so a completely new range was built to service the garden's growing needs. It now requires three full-time staff to run it.

This remarkable recreation has been led by a man who was not previously a walled gardener. David's life and business interests have for many years been focused in the Far East, an influence immediately apparent in his decision to build a tropical greenhouse. Dominated by papaya trees, this also provides a base for nurturing ginger, turmeric, galangal, passion fruit and heliconia. When Watt bought the garden there were no operational glasshouses, only the ruins of a 1908 Foster Pearson greenhouse and the footings of another four, giving him the opportunity to start afresh. The chance find of Andrew Legge, an extraordinary cabinet-maker and craftsman, transformed the project. Tasked with rebuilding and recreating a range of glass buildings, Legge tackled the challenge with initiative, creativity and speed: he rebuilt the Foster Pearson house as it had been in an astonishing six weeks, exactly matching his estimated time and budget. Legge now continues to transform other features on the wider estate, in a role has become virtually full-time.

Since that first project, many more glasshouses have been added. All are built from Western Red Cedar, including a sunken propagating house with brick-built and heated beds, topped with a full-length cantilevered ridge ventilator as its crowning glory. Reconstructing the glasshouses so authentically in size and function has been made possible largely through the upcycling of original cast-iron and brass fittings. The numerous levers, pieces of winding gear, hinges and brackets include many original examples salvaged from glasshouses demolished at Westonbirt, Gloucestershire, investing the structures at Newport with a sense that they have always been there.

Newport and its owner are unique. It is certainly not the biggest garden of its kind, nor the most historic in terms of features; so much of that history has been lost or buried. Yet through the careful, ongoing process of reconstruction and redevelopment, its gardeners and the family that it now supports have gained a window into the original walled gardeners' world. Watts and his team have created a space tailored to their needs and, while being sensitive to the garden's history, the lack of extant historic fabric has allowed them considerable freedom. As a result, Newport House and its garden may represent a taste of living history. It is an unexpected, beautiful and revealing glimpse into the secret world of the private walled garden.

OPPOSITE The gardener's bothy is now complete with a thatched roof, conservatory and en-suite facilities that no old gardener could ever have dreamt of, while the extensive glasshouse range beyond boasts a papaya house and propagation house. Reinstated glazed peach screens complete the picture of a meticulously thorough renovation.

GRAVETYE MANOR

West Sussex

Gravetye Manor in West Sussex is an Elizabethan gem that has overlooked its surrounding 1,000 acres (405ha) since 1598. As an architectural treat this alone would recommend it, but for those interested in walled gardens its riches are unique.

Like most manor houses from the period, it would once have had a modest kitchen garden adjacent to the house. There may still be a hint of this earlier enclosure beneath the rich stone terracing and sumptuous grounds that both surround and define the house. Yet really to make sense of Gravetye you need to turn to the late nineteenth century. Then it became the home of William Robinson, since described as the father of the English flower garden. From humble Irish beginnings Robinson rose to become one of the foremost gardeners of his day. His career made him not only a small fortune as an author, but also something of a celebrity; it also secured his reputation as a plantsman, environmentalist, garden designer and, according to some, a maverick.

Robinson bought the Gravetye estate in 1884. Over the next 50 years it became his horticultural canvas, upon which he developed and demonstrated his ideas. Elaborate terracing and the framing of the manor in a mass of planting – or 'wild planting', as he described it – allowed Robinson to surround himself with what to many is a quintessential English flower garden. He also turned his attention to the existing walled garden. In the best traditions

of eighteenth-century landscapers he started again, creating a new enclosure worthy of such an inventive spirit. The result, completed in 1901, was a unique elliptical garden, built entirely from the sandstone that gives the manor its distinctive golden hue, which was quarried from the estate.

Gravetye is now perhaps better known as one of Britain's most exclusive country hotels, possessing a Michelin star and a growing global reputation for excellence. Since Robinson's death in 1935, and a brief spell during the war when it housed Canadian troops, it has been developed and maintained as a luxurious retreat through successive owners. Its walled garden has enjoyed mixed fortunes, but is today fully productive again. The garden is at the heart of Gravetye's menu, thanks to the efforts of head gardener Tom Coward and renowned head chef George Blogg.

The walled kitchen garden here is fascinating for several reasons, especially its shape, aspect, elevation and the materials from which it is built. It may not be the biggest in the country, nor does it have all the features that many possess. However, its elliptical layout and elevation have helped to create a unique growing environment, as Tom and his assistant Helena explained on a warm late March day.

The camera's lens accentuates the unique properties and layout of Gravetye Manor's elliptical walled kitchen garden, once again bursting with produce that underwrites head chef George Blogg's well-deserved Michelin Star.

The first thing you notice on the way to the kitchen garden is its position: set on top of a small hill, it enjoys a south-facing aspect. Robinson was constrained in where he could site his new creation. We know from his notes that the original square garden was probably on the site of the current stone terrace, today one of Gravetye's most cherished features. It appears that Robinson filled in and raised the level of the old walled garden to create the terrace, in time extending it to create the base for his summer-house and an arbour that now gives the far side of this garden its distinctive backdrop. In siting the new kitchen garden, it occurred to Robinson that an elliptical shape was not only the most practical, but would also create a different dynamic within the space.

The chill of the morning air began to lift as I approached the huge gates at its southern end. 'We often find that the garden inside the walls is three weeks ahead of the rest of the estate,' Tom explained. 'The old man knew that hot air rises and cold air sinks. Perched on this elevated position, the garden makes the best of that, while the curved walls capture the passage of the sun throughout the day.' From the centre, the true scale and unique aspect of the kitchen garden becomes apparent. Sweeping around either side, embracing the neat beds that filled every inch of this now very productive space, the ellipse Robinson created has a captivating effect.

Traditionally one of the kitchen garden's defining elements was its ability to produce food all year round, whether freshly picked or sourced from the stores. Even in late March swathes of leeks were ready to go, while a recent initiative to pickle certain crops ensures

OPPOSITE Well-used forcers line up in the rhubarb patch.
PAGES 222–223 The walled garden in late spring.

LEFT The original kitchen garden was retained by this terrace and overlooked by the manor, as was typical during the Elizabethan period when gardens were designed to be adjacent to their houses.

that some of the garden's finest produce is available all year. Tom and his team have come to relish the challenge of supplying the best seasonal ingredients to a Michelin-starred restaurant. Their relationship with chef George Blogg has evolved into a great creative partnership, with a list of 'must haves' and 'would like to have' being supplied every evening. The gardeners do their best to gather what is available in the morning, allowing time to amend the menu if necessary. Tom acknowledges that they occasionally spot a chef running around the garden in search of more supplies. 'It's great to see, and for guests to see too,' he laughed. 'It proves the value of what we are doing and how fresh our menu is.'

For George, whose determination to provide a seasonal menu has helped gain the chef his Michelin

In Robinson's day, the glasshouse company Foster and Pearson were the market leaders. Gravetye retains several fine examples.

star, the garden's value is immeasurable. 'In pure economic terms, the figures may not always add up,' he explained. 'But can you put a price on freshness? Yes, we could order in whatever I chose to cook, and we'd get it from all over the world at any time of year, but here my cooking is dictated by the garden and what's in season. That means I have a tougher job, constantly tweaking and adapting the menu day after day, but that pairing between the kitchen and the garden is what makes us unique. When I interview new chefs I often do it in the walled garden. If they're not interested in what we're doing it's obvious, and it's clear that Gravetye isn't for them.'

Attention to detail is as important here today as when Robinson was in charge. Yet two key features are noticeably absent within Gravetye's enchanting ellipse. The first is the lack of a central dipping pond. One of the reasons Robinson chose the site was the presence of a natural spring, which he incorporated into a pool at a point alongside the eastern boundary. The second glaring omission is glasshouses. These would have been a challenge to build against the walls, given there is not a single straight line in sight. The exterior of the wall is thus unencumbered with bothies, boiler rooms or stores, leaving the graceful lines of this unique enclosure true to their original design.

Robinson's solution was to build a series of seven Foster and Pearson glasshouses 200 yards away from the garden, perfectly positioned on a south-westerly-facing slope. Now restored, they include a stunning peach house, where figs are trained on the wall, and a range of cold frames with their original winding gear and fittings – all full to the brim with stock for both garden and kitchen.

Robinson's garden is as original as he was. Never shy of breaking with tradition in his passionate pursuit of naturalistic gardening, he created a kitchen garden which is genuinely unique and sought to make the best of its position and purpose. Built during the twilight years of the walled garden, its simplicity proved its strength. Gravetye's position as a centre of horticultural and culinary excellence is a striking legacy for a man whose innovation and imagination came to define the very idea of the English garden.

This simple inscription perhaps belies the rather complex personality behind Gravetye's transformation at the turn of the twentieth century.

GORDON CASTLE

Moray

'Everything presents the appearance of skillful and successful management, and gives much pleasure to all who have the good fortune to visit the gardens.'
Gardeners' Magazine, 1903

For over 400 years Gordon Castle in Moray has been home to the Dukes of Gordon and Richmond. At its peak the estate covered some 330,000 acres (133.54ha), while the family's interests extended to include among others, Goodwood House in Sussex. During the late fifteenth century the original castle, complete with a striking six-storey tower, was built on marshy ground known locally as the Bog of Gight. The castle was framed with formal gardens typical of the period, including at least one kitchen garden, along with a series of canals, orchards and avenues. In the second half of the eighteenth century the trend for 'improved' landscapes resulted in the wholesale rebuilding of the castle and a radical redesign of its grounds. The new castle, a beautiful, sprawling, neoclassical mansion, was symmetrically centred on the original tower, now looking over a landscaped park. The scheme also required the neighbouring village of Fochabers to be demolished and rebuilt a discreet distance to the south, giving the house and its owners uninterrupted views in every direction.

The castle's walled kitchen garden was also improved. The original, close to the house, may by this time have become too small, and its fabric was probably in need of repair. The flood plain to the south extends to a long east–west ridge, upon which the village had previously stood. Now cleared, the site was eventually chosen for a new kitchen

OPPOSITE This huge garden, developed by designer Arne Maynard, contains a series of areas that are both purposeful and playful, combining a traditional kitchen garden with landforms and a maze.

BELOW Given the size of the garden, it's almost impossible to capture all of it on camera unless from the air.

garden that would come to rival the finest in Britain, not just in terms of production, but also of scale. Records of wages and materials suggest that it was built between 1803–4. The result was a staggering 8 acre (3.2ha) garden, fitting for a country seat that by the turn of the twentieth century needed a staff of 150 to run it. The garden's great brick walls enclosed a classic layout of quadrants and beds bursting with produce. The walls were also covered with hundreds of fruit trees, both inside and out.

Today the estate is run by Zara and Angus Gordon Lennox. Changing family fortunes forced the sale of the castle in 1937, after which it was requisitioned for the war effort – a period that saw a rapid deterioration in the fabric of the building. In 1953 Angus's grandfather managed to buy back the now-dilapidated castle and part of the estate within its parkland walls. Sadly much of the original building had to be demolished, but its eastern range and the historic tower remained. A thorough trawl through the archives, both in Moray and in Edinburgh, has revealed much about the historic development of the garden. It has now set the scene for a radical redesign and renovation that, when complete, will give Gordon Castle one of Britain's biggest productive kitchen gardens.

Yet just four years ago the garden was empty, its once prodigious beds and borders left to grass and once orderly quadrants erased from view. As the Gordon Lennoxes will testify, running an estate such as theirs is always a financial tightrope. Diversification is key to meeting this challenge and the walled garden is now central to that strategy, assisted by the foresight of their ancestors.

One vital factor was the diligence of the oldest member of the estate's team. Since 1947 Willie Robertson, the now retired head gardener, had dutifully cared for the 259 fruit trees covering the walls. Long after the kitchen garden had been left to grass Robertson still tended and pruned them, his efforts rewarded year after year with a spectacular crop of apples, pears, plums and figs. Most was sadly

OPPOSITE The Head Gardener's house feels a little out of place in the middle of a Scottish estate. It's thought its design was influenced by the architecture of West Sussex that surrounded the family's other former home at Goodwood House.

LEFT Scabious and daffodils are just some of several thousand trees and plants that have been brought in to fill the garden.

229

The enormous Gordon Castle walled garden has plenty of space for a huge range of flowers and vegetables, which are used in the estate's award-winning café.

unused and wasted until the Gordon Lennoxes began to wonder whether this rich harvest might help to secure the future of the estate.

In 2011 they started to produce herbs and other botanical plants from which to extract essential oils for a growing range of bath and beauty products. Large areas to the west of the walled garden were sown, with planting including lavender, chamomile and rosemary. An old whisky still was adapted for use in extracting the oils needed. The turning point came with the realisation that not only did the huge garden make perfect growing space for the herbs, but its fruit crop could also, quite literally, be pressed into service. The eureka moment emerged through the subsequent plan to renovate the garden as a venue, to showcase where their growing range of products was sourced.

The ambition to garden 8 acres (3.2ha) was a huge gamble. As Zara Gordon Lennox explained, 'Angus always said that the garden was too big for the house, but too small for Tesco. In other words, if it was to work it would have to be on its own terms.' Seeking to develop a venue that was both productive and attractive was no small challenge. Eventually designer Arne Maynard was invited to reimagine the garden and architect Craig Hamilton enlisted to develop an award-winning café on the site of the old glasshouses.

In 2012 reconstruction of the garden began. Arne's design, due to be completed in 2018/19, is already delivering very impressive results. He and Craig have set out a bold garden, mixing contemporary planting with an imaginative approach to space. Where only recently there was simply grass, the walled garden now includes a sunken theatre, several striking, crescent-shaped landforms and a maze, in a garden that will, in time, be divided with hundreds of new espaliered fruit trees. These vertical screens will help to manage the air flow within its vast acreage, in so doing creating planting rooms that afford some protection to the beds they surround. In addition to the 259 trained trees cared for so expertly by Willie Robertson, over 1,000 new ones have now been planted.

The scale of what they have embarked upon has been remarkable. Zara Gordon Lennox admits that at the outset they did not quite appreciate just how much time, effort and materials would be involved. Over 1½ miles (2.5km) of pathways have been laid, edged with 48,000 handmade bricks, all planted with at least 30,000 new plants, from cut flowers to herbs and vegetable stock that is constantly being added to. There is no doubt that if the owners and their small but dedicated team had not been so hands-on, this would have been an impossible task. One thing this garden does not lack is the need for hard physical work. Everything is done by hand, the only concessions to modern life being a tractor and trailer.

Key appointments to the project included head gardener John Hawley and his colleague Ed Bollom, both of whom leapt at the chance to help create the garden from the outset. 'The chance to get involved

from the beginning is every walled gardener's dream,' confided John, whose 20-year career has included some equally demanding gardens, such as Sizergh in Cumbria. 'Getting to grips with Arne's plan, and transferring that from paper into the growing reality you see today has been fascinating,' he explained. 'From the hard landscaping to the planting scheme, seeing this astonishing space come

back to life in a form that combines the best of the old with a keen eye on the future is to me what makes this place so special.'

Gordon Castle is now a brand in its own right, with an expanding range of products and produce originating from within its extensive, once empty, walled garden. There is no doubt that it has required enormous energy and investment, but Zara Gordon Lennox is optimistic about the future. 'We have a long way to go, and a lot more work to do, but year on year we are getting there.' A gamble it may have been, but great vision, creativity and hard work have produced an extraordinary outcome. In giving new life to a once forgotten gem, the team have transformed it into possibly the biggest and most productive walled kitchen garden in the country.

LEFT Head Gardener Willy Robertson as a young apprentice outside the original Mackenzie and Moncur glasshouse, which has recently been restored.

ABOVE In common with many walled gardens, the one at Gordon Castle incorporates a small dipping pond among the flower beds.

GARDENS TO VISIT

Acorn Bank
Temple Sowerby, near Penrith,
Cumbria CA10 1SP
www.nationaltrust.org.uk/
acorn-bank

Acton Scott
near Church Stretton,
Shropshire SY6 6QQ
actonscott.com

**Arlington Court and the National
Trust Carriage Museum**
Arlington, near Barnstaple,
Devon EX31 4LP
www.nationaltrust.org.uk/
arlington-court-and-the-national-
trust-carriage-museum

Attingham Park
Atcham, Shrewsbury, Shropshire
SY4 4TP
www.nationaltrust.org.uk/
attingham-park

Baddesley Clinton
Rising Lane, Baddesley Clinton,
Warwickshire B93 0DQ
www.nationaltrust.org.uk/
baddesley-clinton

Barrington Court
Barrington, near Ilminster,
Somerset TA19 0NQ
www.nationaltrust.org.uk/
barrington-court

Bateman's
Bateman's Lane, Burwash,
East Sussex TN19 7DS
www.nationaltrust.org.uk/
batemans

**Beningbrough Hall, Gallery
and Gardens**
Beningbrough, York,
North Yorkshire YO30 1DD
www.nationaltrust.org.uk/
beningbrough-hall-gallery-
and-gardens

Berrington Hall
near Leominster,
Herefordshire HR6 0DW
www.nationaltrust.org.uk/
berrington-hall

Bicton Park Botanical Gardens
East Budleigh, Budleigh Salterton,
Exeter, Devon EX9 7BJ
www.bictongardens.co.uk

Blickling Estate
Blickling, Aylsham,
Norfolk NR11 6NF
www.nationaltrust.org.uk/
blickling-estate

Calke Abbey
Ticknall, Derby,
Derbyshire DE73 7LE
www.nationaltrust.org.uk/
calke-abbey

Chartwell
Mapleton Road, Westerham,
Kent TN16 1PS
www.nationaltrust.org.uk/
chartwell

Chastleton House
Chastleton, near Moreton-in-
Marsh, Oxfordshire GL56 0SU
www.nationaltrust.org.uk/
chastleton-house

Chatsworth House
Chatsworth, Bakewell,
Derbyshire DE45 1PP
www.chatsworth.org

Clumber Park
Worksop, Nottinghamshire,
S80 3AZ
www.nationaltrust.org.uk/
clumber-park

Combermere Abbey
Whitchurch, Shropshire SY13 4AJ
combermereabbey.co.uk

Coughton Court
Alcester, Warwickshire B49 5JA
www.nationaltrust.org.uk/
coughton-court

Croft Castle and Parkland
Yarpole, near Leominster,
Herefordshire HR9 9PW
www.nationaltrust.org.uk/
croft-castle-and-parkland

Deans Court
Deans Court Lane, Wimborne,
Dorset BH21 1EE
www.deanscourt.org

Dyffryn Gardens
St Nicholas, Vale of Glamorgan
CF5 6SU
www.nationaltrust.org.uk/
dyffryn-gardens

Easton Walled Gardens
Easton, Grantham,
Lincolnshire NG33 5AP
www.visiteaston.co.uk

Erddig
Wrexham LL13 0YT
www.nationaltrust.org.uk/erddig

Felbrigg Hall, Gardens and Estate
Felbrigg, Norwich,
Norfolk NR11 8PR
www.nationaltrust.org.uk/
felbrigg-hall-gardens-and-estate

Fenton House
Hampstead Grove, London
NW3 6SP
www.nationaltrust.org.uk/
fenton-house-and-garden

**Gravetye Manor Hotel and
Restaurant**
Vowels Lane, West Hoathly,
West Sussex RH19 4LJ
www.gravetyemanor.co.uk

Greys Court
Rotherfield Greys, Henley-on-Thames, Oxfordshire RG9 4PG
www.nationaltrust.org.uk/greys-court

Gordon Castle
Fochabers, Moray IV32 7PQ
www.gordoncastle.co.uk

Greenway
Greenway Road, Galmpton, near Brixham, Devon TQ5 0ES
www.nationaltrust.org.uk/greenway

Hinton Ampner
Hinton Ampner, near Alresford, Hampshire SO24 0LA
www.nationaltrust.org.uk/hinton-ampner

Knightshayes
Bolham, Tiverton, Devon EX16 7RQ
www.nationaltrust.org.uk/knightshayes

Lacock Abbey, Fox Talbot Museum and Village
Lacock, near Chippenham, Wiltshire SN15 2LG
www.nationaltrust.org.uk/lacock-abbey-fox-talbot-museum-and-village

Llanerchaeron
Ciliau Aeron, near Aberaeron, Ceredigion SA48 8DG
www.nationaltrust.org.uk/llanerchaeron

The Lost Gardens of Heligan
Pentewan, St. Austell, Cornwall PL26 6EN
heligan.com

Mottisfont
near Romsey, Hampshire SO51 0LP
www.nationaltrust.org.uk/mottisfont

Normanby Hall Country Park
Normanby, North Lincolnshire DN15 9HU
www.normanbyhall.co.uk

Osterley Park and House
Jersey Road, Isleworth, Middlesex TW7 4RB
www.nationaltrust.org.uk/osterley-park-and-house

Packwood House
Packwood Lane, Lapworth, Warwickshire B94 6AT
www.nationaltrust.org.uk/packwood-house

Scotney Castle
Lamberhurst, Tunbridge Wells, Kent TN3 8JN
www.nationaltrust.org.uk/scotney-castle

Shugborough Estate
Milford, near Stafford, Staffordshire ST17 0XB
www.nationaltrust.org.uk/shugborough-estate

Slebech Park Restaurant and Rooms
Haverfordwest, Pembrokeshire SA62 4AX
www.slebech.co.uk

Stackpole Walled Gardens
Stackpole Estate, Pembroke, Pembrokeshire SA71 5DY
www.stackpole-walledgardens.co.uk

Tatton Park
Knutsford, Cheshire WA16 8QN
www.tattonpark.org.uk

Trengwainton Garden
Madron, near Penzance, Cornwall TR20 8RZ
www.nationaltrust.org.uk/trengwainton-garden

Tyntesfield
Wraxall, Bristol, North Somerset BS48 1NX
www.nationaltrust.org.uk/tyntesfield

Upton House and Gardens
near Banbury, Warwickshire OX15 6HT
www.nationaltrust.org.uk/upton-house-and-gardens

Westbury Court Garden
Westbury-on-Severn, Gloucestershire GL14 1PD
www.nationaltrust.org.uk/westbury-court-garden

West Dean Gardens
West Dean, near Chichester, West Sussex PO18 0RX
www.westdean.org.uk/gardens

Wimpole Estate
Arrington, Royston, Cambridgeshire SG8 0BW
www.nationaltrust.org.uk/wimpole-estate

PICTURE CREDITS

5 © Lorna Tremayne / Heligan Gardens Ltd; 6 (top), 68–69, 82–83 © National Trust Images / Brian and Nina Chapple; 6 (bottom), 20–21, 36–37, 66–67 (top), 77, 92–93, 125, 126, 162, 163, 170 © National Trust Images / Andrew Butler; 7, 142–143 LEE BEEL / Alamy Stock Photo; 9, 31, 67 © National Trust Images / James Dobson; 10, 51, 131 (left) © National Trust Images / Mark Bolton; 12–13 © Vertical Horizons Media, Duncan Hine; 14–15 © National Trust Images / Val Corbett; 18 Pictorial Press Ltd / Alamy Stock Photo; 19, 47 © National Trust Images / John Miller; 22, 112–113, 128, 164–165, 182–183 © National Trust Images / David Dixon; 23 World History Archive / Alamy Stock Photo; 25, 75 © Matthew Hawkey, Heligan Gardens Ltd; 26–27, 48, 134–135, 206 © National Trust Images / Mike Calnan; 30–31, 32 © National Trust Images / Mark Sunderland; 40–41, 44, 58–59 © Julia Lammers; 42–43 © Gravetye Manor; 53 Julian Money-Kyrle / Alamy Stock Photo; 54–55 Bob Gibbons / Alamy Stock Photo; 57 (top), 151 © National Trust Images / Stephen Robson; 63 (left) © National Trust Images / David Levenson; 70–71, 174–175 © National Trust Images / William Shaw; 72–73, 196–197, 198 © Heligan Gardens / James Stephens; 74–75, 131 (bottom right) © National Trust Images / Derek Croucher; 80–81 © National Trust Images / Steve Stephens; 81, 85, 116 (top), 116 (bottom) © National Trust Images / John Millar; 84 (left) © National Trust Images / Geoff Morgan; 84 (right) Heather Drake / Alamy Stock Photo; 88–89, 102, 102–103, 106, 107 © Fred Cholmeley; 91 Chatsworth House, seat of William Cavendish (1640–1707) 1st Duke of Devonshire, engraved by Johannes Kip (c.1652–1722) (engraving), Knyff, Leonard (1650–1721) (after) / Private Collection / The Stapleton Collection / Bridgeman Images; 108–109 Garden World Images Ltd / Alamy Stock Photo; 115, 133, 120, 202 © National Trust Images / David Sellman; 129 (bottom) © National Trust Images / Ian Shaw; 136–137 (top) Herefordshire Archives and Record Centre; 136–137 (bottom) © Combermere Abbey; 140 Heritage Image Partnership Ltd / Alamy Stock Photo; 144–145 © National Trust Images / Paul Mogford; 146 © National Trust Images / Jerry Harpur; 149 (left, top right and bottom right), 150 © National Trust Images / David Noton; 155 John Keates / Alamy Stock Photo; 156 allotment boy 1 / Alamy Stock Photo; 157 (bottom left) The National Trust Photolibrary / Alamy Stock Photo; 158 (bottom) © Tatton Park / Cheshire East Council / Peter Spooner; 158–159 © National Trust Images / Robert Morris; 160–161 UK City Images / Alamy Stock Photo; 171 John Glover / Alamy Stock Photo; 174, 176, 178 © National Trust Images / Paul Harris; 184–185, 200, 204–205, 207 ©National Trust Images / Claire Takacs; 186 Archives and Special Collections, Bangor University, Bangor, Plas Newydd VIII 5013; 192 © Toby Strong, Heligan Gardens Ltd; 192–193 garfotos / Alamy Stock Photo; 194 Skim New Media Limited / Alamy Stock Photo; 195 Carolyn Eaton / Alamy Stock Photo; 196 roger holfert / Alamy Stock Photo; 203 ZUMA Press, Inc. / Alamy Stock Photo; 210–211 © Claire Takacs; 218–219, 222–223 © Mimi Connolly. All other images © Jules Hudson.

FURTHER READING

Much of this book owes its content to the many gardeners, plantsmen and women who gave of their time so readily and with such enthusiasm in showing me their gardens. Whatever the weather and without haste, they shared what they knew and often indulged my further suggestions and interpretations of the gardens they care for. I am indebted to the following authors for their excellent studies to which I have often referred.

Browse, Philip McMillan, *Heligan: Fruit, Flowers and Herbs* (Alison Hodges, 2005)

Buczacki, Stefan, *Churchill & Chartwell* (Frances Lincoln, 2007)

Campbell, Susan, *A History of Kitchen Gardening* (Unicorn, 2015)

Campbell, Susan, *Walled Kitchen Gardens* (Shire Publications, 2006)

Eburne, Andrew, *The Walled Garden*, Blickling Hall, Norfolk (conservation statement for the National Trust, 2008)

Gammack, Helene, *The Kitchen Garden Estate* (National Trust, 2012)

Grant, Fiona, *Glasshouses* (Shire Publications, 2013)

Hill, Thomas, *The Gardener's Labyrinth*, with an introduction by Richard Mabey (Oxford University Press, 1987)

Musgrave, Toby, *The Head Gardeners, Forgotten Heroes of Horticulture* (Aurum Press, 2009)

Robinson, William, *The Wild Garden* (Timber Press, 2009)

Rutherford, Sarah, *Capability Brown & His Landscape Gardens* (National Trust Books, 2016)

Rutherford, Sarah, Plas Newydd, Anglesey. *Historic Landscape Analysis* (National Trust, 2009)

Saville, Diana, *Walled Gardens, their planting and design* (Batsford, 1992)

Smit, Tim, *The Lost Gardens of Heligan* (Orion, 2000)

Watson, William, *The Gardener's Assistant* (Gresham Publishing Co., 1925, vols I–V)

Wilson, C. Anne. (ed.), *The Country House Kitchen Garden, 1600–1950* (The History Press, 2010)

Wood, Eric. S., *Historical Britain* (Harvill, 1995)

INDEX

ACKNOWLEDGEMENTS

When coming to the end of writing a book on such a fascinating subject, the final pleasure is undoubtedly having the chance to thank a great many people without whom its production would not have been possible.

I start with Harvey Edgington, a long-term associate who traditionally sorts out our access for filming at National Trust properties. It was on his recommendation that the Trust's Publisher, Katie Bond, made contact, from which followed a meeting with her publishing partner at Pavilion Books, Peter Taylor. I remain extremely grateful to them both for agreeing to take on a rookie writer and commission *Walled Gardens*. Not only did they share my enthusiasm for the idea, they also conferred on me complete freedom of thought in devising the format and content, and were wonderfully patient and ever-supportive of my endless deliberations.

Having set out the structure, my next task was to go about selecting and visiting those featured gardens that make up the book. My first stop was to Susan Campbell, whose reputation in the study of walled kitchen gardens preceded her. She was wonderfully supportive and insightful, and over lunch in Hampshire advised me to write the book that I wanted to write, and so it has turned out. What followed was a year-long odyssey that took me all over the country. Those gardens, their gardeners and owners are well documented in the text, but I should like to reiterate my unending thanks for the very gracious time, patience and enthusiasm that they all shared with characteristic charm and warmth. Every visit revealed something new to us all, and they remain without doubt the highlight of the adventure as time spent in magical surroundings, and always with the most inspiring company.

I was also helped with some additional research by long-term family friend, neighbour and brilliant gardener Mandy Green, who shared my passion for the subject and gave up much of her precious time. However, when all was done and dusted, it fell to my editor, Nicola Newman at Pavilion, to help make sense of the 60 thousand words and over three thousand pictures that I delivered to her on a bulging memory stick. Her patience and creative flair, combined with a keen eye on maintaining my vision and the character of the book, made the process of converting my thoughts into visual reality a genuine and collaborative pleasure. Gemma Doyle, the talented designer on the book, found Julia Lammers, a young Austrian artist based in Vienna, who has provided the illustrations that so eloquently help to describe the fantasy walled garden in the opening chapters, and who expertly translated my sketches and notes.

My final thanks must go to my wife, Tania. Armed with the forensic mind of an accomplished Finance Director, she ably and succinctly provided much invaluable input on those early drafts and the book's developing structure, ensuring that it has emerged I hope as an accessible, colourful and engaging work that does justice to these enchanting and rather magical gardens.

First published in the United Kingdom in 2018 by
National Trust Books
43 Great Ormond Street
London
WC1N 3HZ

An imprint of Pavilion Books Company Ltd

ISBN 978-1-90988-196-9

A CIP catalogue record for this book is available from the British Library.

10 9 8 7 6 5 4 3 2

Reproduction by Rival Colour Ltd, UK
Printed and bound by GPS Group, Slovenia

This book can be ordered direct from the publisher at www.pavilionbooks.com